COLORADO
BIKING
TRAILS

DISCLAIMER
Information contained in this guide is for trip planning and general reference only. Use good judgement when planning a trip. Trail ratings and
directions are general guides, physical condition, age, weather, elevation,
and experience are factors that should be considered. If you have concerns
or questions about conditions or routes contact the agency that manages the
area you are going to visit. The intended use of this guide is for trip planning only. Outdoor Books & Maps is not responsible for mishap or injury
from the use of this guide.

ISBN 0-930657-28-4

© Copyright 1998-2007 Outdoor Books & Maps

This publication cannot be reproduced in whole or in part without
written permission from Adler Publishing Company, Inc.

3 1813 00344 4790

Outdoor Books & Maps
An imprint of Adler Publishing Company, Inc.
P.O. Box 519
Castle Rock, CO 80104
Phone: (800) 660-5107
Fax (303) 688-4388

COLORADO
BIKING
TRAILS

OUTDOOR BOOKS

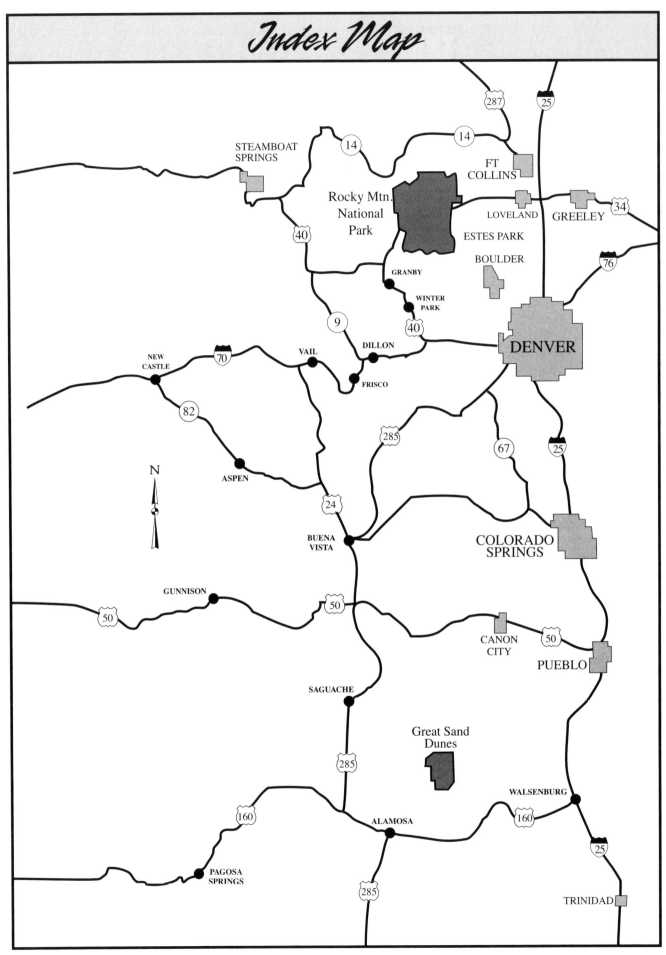

TABLE OF CONTENTS

INTRODUCTION   6

HOW TO USE THIS GUIDE   6

ASPEN REGION MAP   **7**
1. Government Trail   8
2. Lincoln Creek Road   9
3. Little Annie Road Loop   10
4. Owl Creek Road   11
5. Rio Grande Trail   12
6. Smuggler Mountain Road/Hunter Creek Loop   13

BOULDER REGION MAP   **15**
7. Fourth of July   16
8. Jamestown   17
9. Lefthand Canyon   18
10. Meyers Gulch   19
11. Sourdough Trail   20
12. Switzerland Trail   21
13. St. Vrain Mountain Trail   22
14. Walker Ranch   23
15. White Ranch   24

COLORADO SPRINGS REGION MAP   **25**
16. New Santa Fe Trail   26
17. Palmer/Redrock Loop   27
18. Rampart Reservoir   28

COLORADO SPRINGS/DENVER REGION MAP   29
19. Buffalo Creek/Colorado Trail   30
20. Morrison/Tramway Creek Loop   31
21. Stoney Pass   32
22. Waterton Canyon   33

DENVER REGION MAP   **35**
23. Apex Park   36
24. Chatfield Reservoir Loop   37
25. Cherry Creek Bike Path   38
26. Dakota Ridge Trail   39
27. Elk Meadow Park   40
28. Golden Gate Canyon   41
29. Matthews/Winter Park   42
30. Mount Falcon   43
31. Mountain Lion/Golden Gate State Park   44
32. Red Rocks Trail   45

ESTES PARK REGION MAP   **47**
33. Crosier Mountain   48
34. House Rock   49
35. Pierson Park   50
36. Pole Hill   51

FORT COLLINS REGION MAP   **53**
37. Foothills Trail   54
38. Hewlett Gulch   55
39. Horsetooth Rock Trail   56
40. Red Feather Lakes Loop   57

SAGUACHE REGION MAP   **59**
41. Archuleta Creek   60
42. Bonita Hill   61
43. California Gulch   62
44. Kerber Creek   63
45. Luder's Creek   64
46. Mosquito Lake   65
47. Mountain Lion Creek   66
48. Round Mountain   67
49. Ute Pass   68

STEAMBOAT SPRINGS REGION MAP   **69**
50. Buffalo Park Road   70
51. Fish Creek Falls   71
52. Lynx Pass   72
53. Rabbit Ears Peak   73
54. Steamboat to Steamboat Lake State Park   74

SUMMIT COUNTY REGION MAP   **75**
55. Boreas Pass Road   76
56. Burro Trail/Mayflower Lake   77
57. Dillon-Keystone Trail   78
58. Gold Run Gulch   79
59. Peaks Trail   80
60. Sally Barber Mine   81

VAIL REGION MAP   **83**
61. Berry Creek Gulch   84
62. Camp Hale to Ptarmigan Pass   85
63. Davos Trail   86
64. Homestake Reservoir   87
65. Lost Lake   88
66. Meadow Mountain   89
67. Mill Creek   90
68. Piney Lake   91
69. Two Elk   92
70. Vail Pass to Red Cliff   93
71. Vail Pass Ten Mile Canyon Nat. Rec. Trail   94
72. Village Trail and Grand Traverse   95

WINTER PARK REGION MAP   **97**
73. Arapaho Trail   98
74. Creekside/Flume/Chainsaw   99
75. Long Trail   100
76. Roof of the Rockies   101
77. Tipperary Creek Loop   102

INDEX   **103**

INTRODUCTION

This book contains 77 of Colorado's best bike rides for all skill levels, from casual rides through the city, scenic rides on mountain two-lane roads or the challenge of single track. The Colorado Biking Trails are within a short driving distance of the front range, included are urban bike paths, scenic mountain roads, single track mountain trails, local conditioning rides, and manicured trails in four major ski areas. These rides were selected by consensus of knowledgeable bicyclists, local chambers of commerce, and forest service personnel as the best bike rides in Colorado.

HOW TO USE THIS GUIDE

This guide is arranged in an easy-to-use format and divided into 12 sections. In the beginning of each section is an index map that locates the trails. Each trail has a locator map, directions to reach the trail, description of ride, general notes, ride profile, and a quick reference information box.

Each trail's quick reference information box describes:

Distance:	**6.0 miles**
Time:	**2.5 hours**
Elevation Gain:	**1200 feet**
Difficulty:	**Moderate**
Surface:	**Gravel road**

Distance: Total miles to complete described ride.

Time: Approximate elapsed time to complete ride.

Elevation Gain: Elevation gain shown in feet from the lowest to the highest point of the ride.

Difficulty: Difficulty of ride for an average bicyclist.

Surface: Road or trail surface of ride.

Ride Profile: Silhouette of trail with distance, reference points and elevation

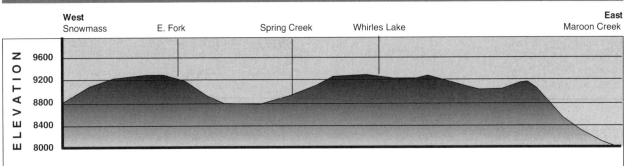

Aspen Area

Rich in mining history, the Aspen area has over 100 miles of trails suitable for mountain bikes and may be the most beautiful place to mountain bike. Biking the low elevation trails, one has the opportunity to view and visit the history of the within the city, while taking the higher elevations provides one the chance to visit old mining sites that once thrived during the late 1800's.

Six trails, popular with local bicyclists, challenge the beginner to the advanced biker: Rio Grande Trail, Smuggler-Hunter Creek Loop, Midnight Mine Road/Little Annie Road, Owl Creek Road, Lincoln Creek Road, and the Government Trail. These trails vary from difficulty to length, depending on the route one chooses.

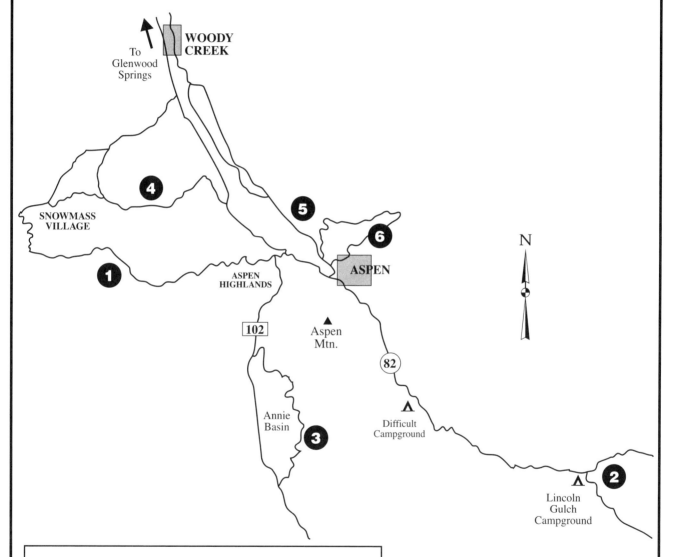

Trail	Page
1. Government Trail	8
2. Lincoln Creek Road	9
3. Little Annie Road Loop	10
4. Owl Creek Road	11
5. Rio Grande Trail	12
6. Smuggler Mtn. Rd./Hunter Creek Loop	13

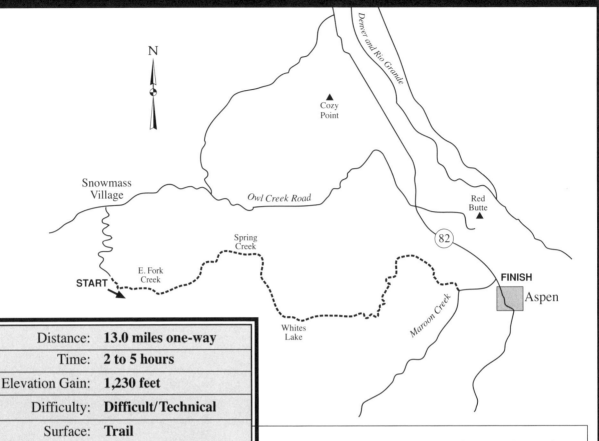

Distance:	**13.0 miles one-way**
Time:	**2 to 5 hours**
Elevation Gain:	**1,230 feet**
Difficulty:	**Difficult/Technical**
Surface:	**Trail**

■ Directions: From Snowmass take Woods Road to Pine Lane, follow Pine Lane to where it dead ends. Pass through the gate onto the ski area and across the ski slopes to a gate. This is the ski area boundary and the start of Government Trail (aka Brush Creek Trail). Look for a Forest Service sign directing you to Buttermilk.

■ Ride: From Snowmass Village take the steep ride up Wood Road to the end where a ski service road leads to Pine Lane then to the Government Trail (also known as Brush Creek Trail). The first part of the trail has several stream crossings and muddy sections before a gentler section in the woods. Be sure to stay above Whites Lake before the Owl Creek crossing. The trail crosses the West Buttermilk ski slopes and the Tiehack Ski Area before dropping steeply to a bridge over Maroon Creek. After a short, steep climb up from the other side of the creek, the trail ends at Iselin Park. From here you can follow the bike path along Maroon Creek Road into Aspen.

■ Notes: Stay on the trail, parts of the trail crosses through private property. Contact the Forest Service for information on trail closures.

Maps: USGS 7.5' Highland Peak and Aspen Quads.
Information: White River National Forest, Aspen Ranger District, (970) 925-3445.

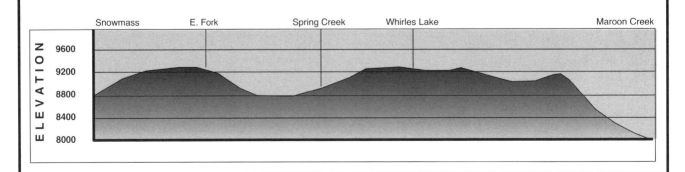

2. Lincoln Creek Road

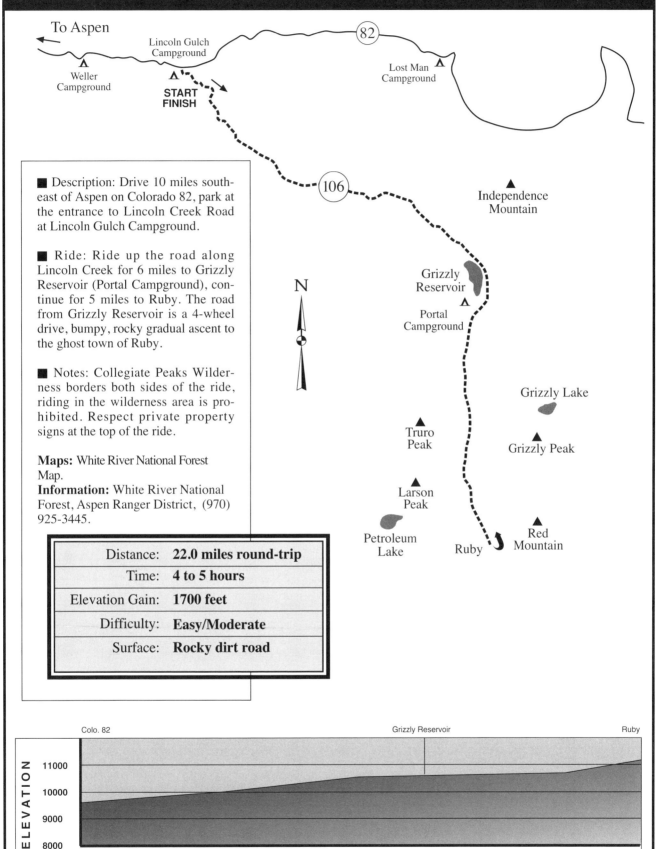

■ Description: Drive 10 miles southeast of Aspen on Colorado 82, park at the entrance to Lincoln Creek Road at Lincoln Gulch Campground.

■ Ride: Ride up the road along Lincoln Creek for 6 miles to Grizzly Reservoir (Portal Campground), continue for 5 miles to Ruby. The road from Grizzly Reservoir is a 4-wheel drive, bumpy, rocky gradual ascent to the ghost town of Ruby.

■ Notes: Collegiate Peaks Wilderness borders both sides of the ride, riding in the wilderness area is prohibited. Respect private property signs at the top of the ride.

Maps: White River National Forest Map.
Information: White River National Forest, Aspen Ranger District, (970) 925-3445.

Distance:	**22.0 miles round-trip**
Time:	**4 to 5 hours**
Elevation Gain:	**1700 feet**
Difficulty:	**Easy/Moderate**
Surface:	**Rocky dirt road**

3. Little Annie Road Loop

Aspen

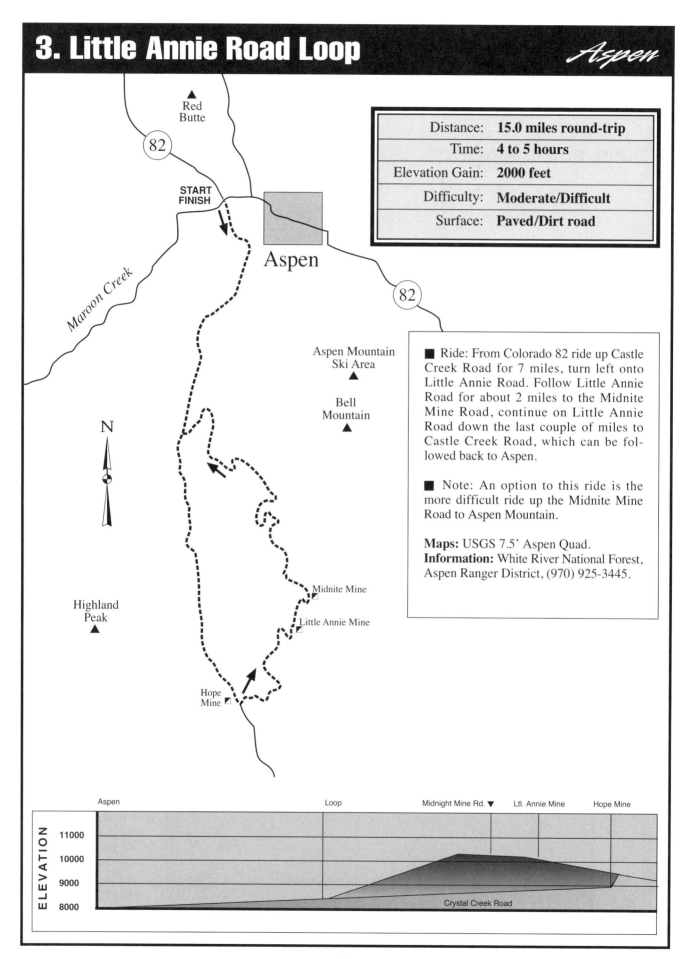

Distance:	**15.0 miles round-trip**
Time:	**4 to 5 hours**
Elevation Gain:	**2000 feet**
Difficulty:	**Moderate/Difficult**
Surface:	**Paved/Dirt road**

Red
Butte

82

START
FINISH

Maroon Creek

Aspen

82

Aspen Mountain
Ski Area
▲

Bell
Mountain
▲

N

Highland
Peak
▲

Midnite Mine

Little Annie Mine

Hope
Mine

■ Ride: From Colorado 82 ride up Castle Creek Road for 7 miles, turn left onto Little Annie Road. Follow Little Annie Road for about 2 miles to the Midnite Mine Road, continue on Little Annie Road down the last couple of miles to Castle Creek Road, which can be followed back to Aspen.

■ Note: An option to this ride is the more difficult ride up the Midnite Mine Road to Aspen Mountain.

Maps: USGS 7.5' Aspen Quad.
Information: White River National Forest, Aspen Ranger District, (970) 925-3445.

Aspen   Loop   Midnight Mine Rd. ▼   Ltl. Annie Mine   Hope Mine

ELEVATION

11000

10000

9000

8000

Crystal Creek Road

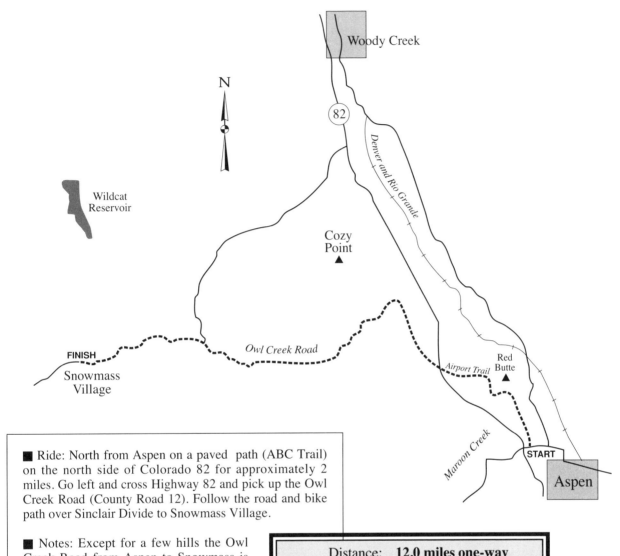

N

Woody Creek

82

Denver and Rio Grande

Wildcat
Reservoir

Cozy
Point
▲

FINISH

Owl Creek Road

Red
Butte
▲

Airport Trail

Snowmass
Village

Maroon Creek

START

Aspen

■ Ride: North from Aspen on a paved path (ABC Trail) on the north side of Colorado 82 for approximately 2 miles. Go left and cross Highway 82 and pick up the Owl Creek Road (County Road 12). Follow the road and bike path over Sinclair Divide to Snowmass Village.

■ Notes: Except for a few hills the Owl Creek Road from Aspen to Snowmass is an easy ride.

Maps: White River National Forest Map.
Information: Aspen Parks & Recreation Department, (970) 920-5120.

Distance:	**12.0 miles one-way**
Time:	**2 to 3 hours**
Elevation Gain:	**580 feet**
Difficulty:	**Moderate**
Surface:	**Paved/Gravel road**

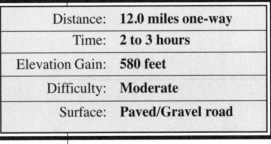

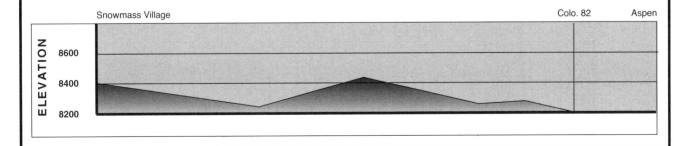

Snowmass Village

Colo. 82

Aspen

ELEVATION

8600

8400

8200

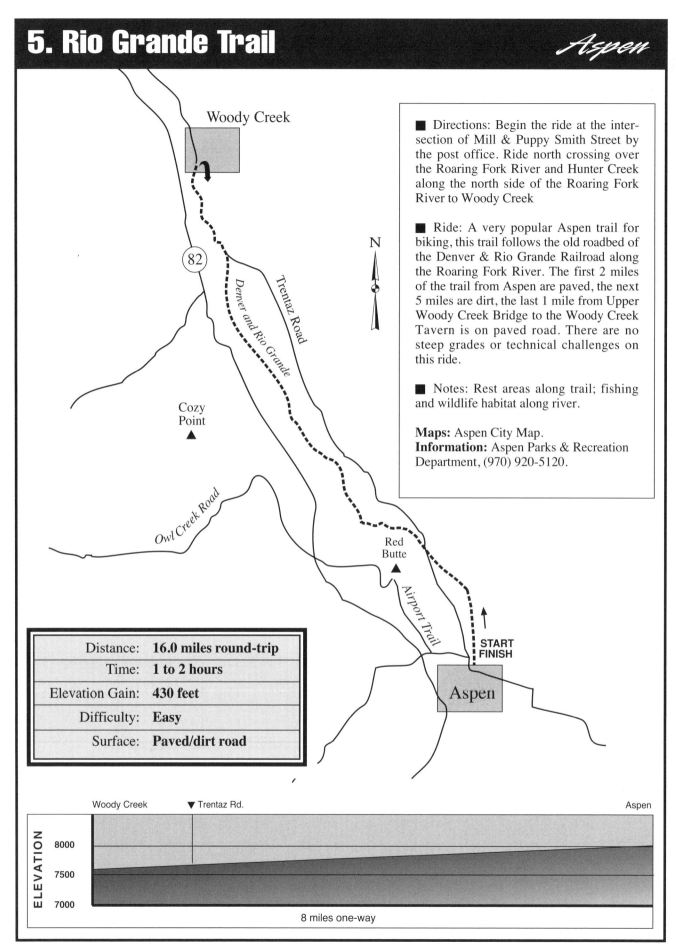

Woody Creek

82

Denver and Rio Grande

Trentaz Road

N

Cozy
Point
▲

Owl Creek Road

Red
Butte
▲

Airport Trail

START
FINISH

Aspen

■ **Directions:** Begin the ride at the intersection of Mill & Puppy Smith Street by the post office. Ride north crossing over the Roaring Fork River and Hunter Creek along the north side of the Roaring Fork River to Woody Creek

■ **Ride:** A very popular Aspen trail for biking, this trail follows the old roadbed of the Denver & Rio Grande Railroad along the Roaring Fork River. The first 2 miles of the trail from Aspen are paved, the next 5 miles are dirt, the last 1 mile from Upper Woody Creek Bridge to the Woody Creek Tavern is on paved road. There are no steep grades or technical challenges on this ride.

■ **Notes:** Rest areas along trail; fishing and wildlife habitat along river.

Maps: Aspen City Map.
Information: Aspen Parks & Recreation Department, (970) 920-5120.

Distance:	**16.0 miles round-trip**
Time:	**1 to 2 hours**
Elevation Gain:	**430 feet**
Difficulty:	**Easy**
Surface:	**Paved/dirt road**

Woody Creek   ▼ Trentaz Rd.   Aspen

ELEVATION

8000

7500

7000

8 miles one-way

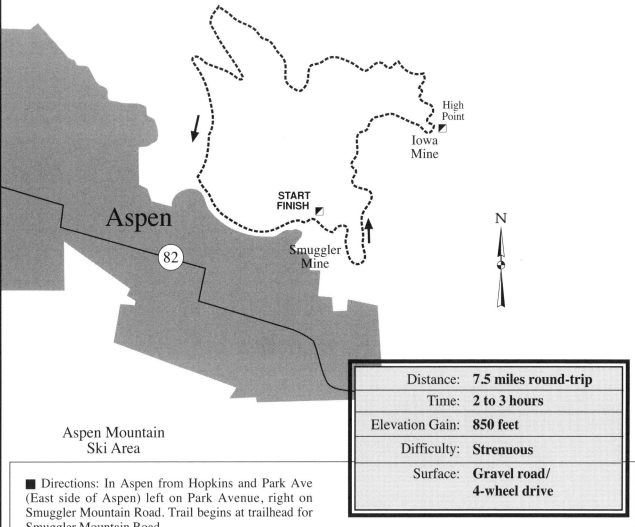

Distance:	**7.5 miles round-trip**
Time:	**2 to 3 hours**
Elevation Gain:	**850 feet**
Difficulty:	**Strenuous**
Surface:	**Gravel road/ 4-wheel drive**

■ Directions: In Aspen from Hopkins and Park Ave (East side of Aspen) left on Park Avenue, right on Smuggler Mountain Road. Trail begins at trailhead for Smuggler Mountain Road.

■ Ride: The first section past the Smuggler mine and up to the Iowa Mine is a series of switchbacks, the road is steep, gravely and rough. From the Iowa Mine the road descends down into the Hunter Valley. Cross the reservoir bridge and turn left, following Hunter Creek down for .75 mile. Stay left and cross the 10 Mountain Bridge; follow the trail down along Hunter Creek. Stay left to Red Mountain Road, and the road will take you back to Aspen.

■ Note: The ride is very strenuous at the beginning and easy on the downside through Hunter Valley.

Maps: White River National Forest Map, USGS 7.5' Aspen and Thimble Rock Quads.
Information: White River National Forest, Aspen Ranger District, (970) 925-3445.

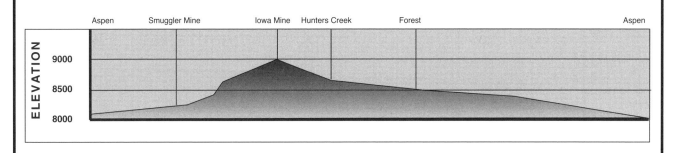

Boulder Area

Trail..**Page**

7. **Fourth of July** **16**
8. **Jamestown** **17**
9. **Lefthand Canyon** **18**
10. **Meyers Gulch** **19**
11. **Sourdough Trail** **20**
12. **Switzerland Trail** **21**
13. **St. Vrain Mountain Trail** **22**
14. **Walker Ranch-Columbine Gulch Loop** ...**23**
15. **White Ranch** **24**

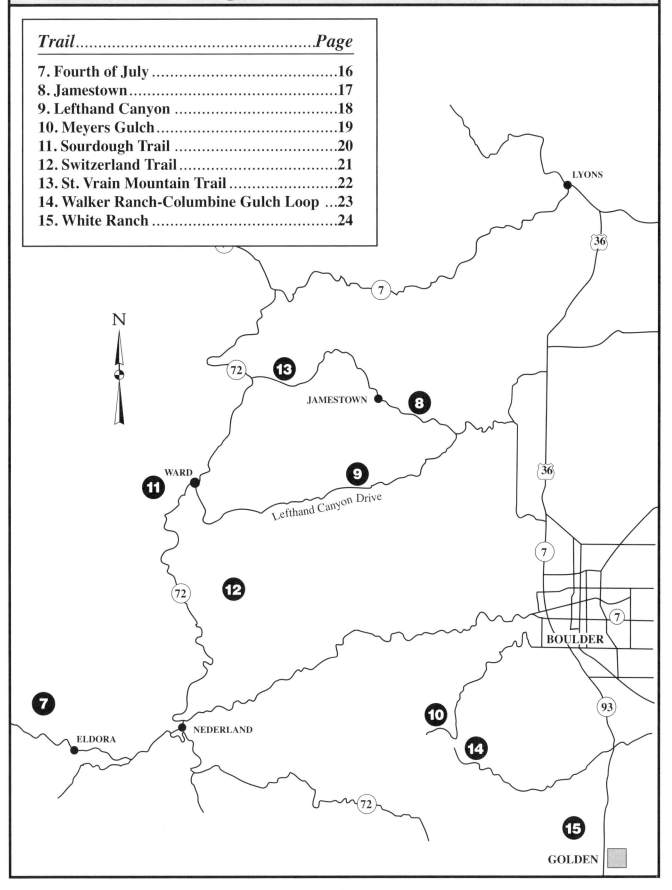

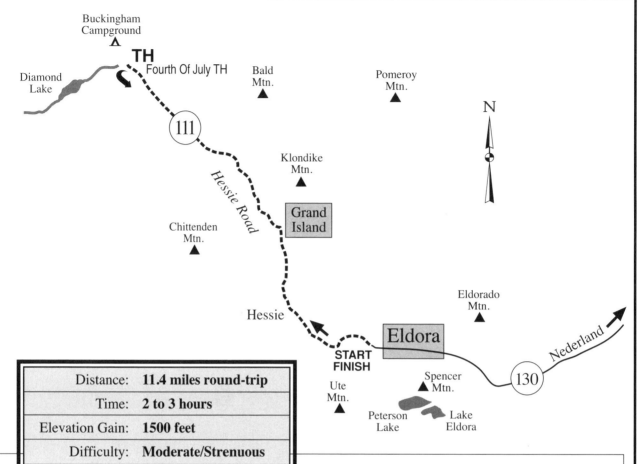

Distance:	**11.4 miles round-trip**
Time:	**2 to 3 hours**
Elevation Gain:	**1500 feet**
Difficulty:	**Moderate/Strenuous**
Surface:	**Gravel road**

■ Directions: From Canyon and Broadway, drive west on Canyon (Hwy 119) to Nederland. From Nederland, bear left on 119 for 0.6 miles to BC Rd. 130, the road to Eldora. Stay right at the turn-off for the Eldora Ski Area and continue for 2.5 miles to the stop sign at 6th Street in the town of Eldora, and park off the road.

■ Ride: Up the Eldora road to the end of the pavement and continue along a dirt road. Stay right at a turn-off for Hessie and climb more steeply. Stay straight on the main road at all junctions. Follow the South Fork of Upper Boulder Creek to the 4th of July Campground at 5.7 miles one-way.

■ Note: Bikes are not allowed in the Indian Peaks Wilderness area beyond the 4th of July Trailhead.

Maps: USGS 7.5' East Portal, Nederland Quads.
Information: Arapaho/Roosevelt National Forest, Boulder Ranger District, (303) 541-2500.

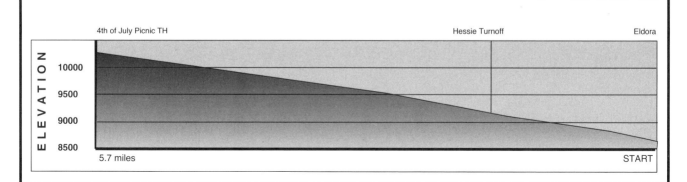

Bald Mtn.

Fairview Peak

START FINISH

Porphyry Mtn.

Bueno Mtn.

Golden Age Hill

36

Jamestown

Buckingham Park

Jamestown Canyon Drive

N

Walker Mtn.

Left Hand Canyon Drive

Lee Hill Road

Old Stage Road

Boulder

■ Directions: From Boulder drive north on US 36 for approximately 3 miles to Lefthand Canyon Drive. There is no designated parking area. Park well off the road.

Ride: Follow Lefthand Canyon upstream along Lefthand Creek approximately 5.5 miles to the turn-off to Jamestown. Turn right and ride 3 miles to Jamestown. The ride is a steady uphill climb with a few steep grades. Shoulders are narrow or non-existent; stay right.

Maps: Arapaho & Roosevelt National Forest Map.
Information: Arapaho/Roosevelt National Forest, Boulder Ranger District, (303) 541-2500.

Distance:	**17.0 miles round-trip**
Time:	**2 to 3 hours**
Elevation Gain:	**1340 feet**
Difficulty:	**Moderate**
Surface:	**Paved**

Jamestown	Lefthand Canyon	Buckingham Park	U.S. 36

ELEVATION

7000

6000

5000

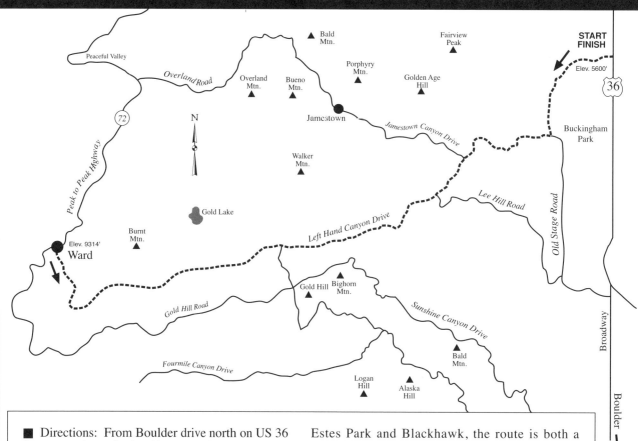

■ Directions: From Boulder drive north on US 36 for approximately 3 miles to Lefthand Canyon Drive. There is no designated parking area. Park well off the road.

■ Ride: Lefthand Canyon is a twisting mountain road that follows Lefthand Creek upstream from Boulder to Ward at Colorado 72. The 16 mile ride is a fairly even climb, except as you approach Ward. Here the climb gets more difficult. The shoulders are typical of mountain county roads, very narrow to non-existent; stay to the right. The ride ends in Ward at Colorado 72.

■ Note: The Peak to Peak Scenic Byway runs directly through Ward. The byway consists of Colorado highways 7, 72, 119. Running between Estes Park and Blackhawk, the route is both a National and State Scenic Byway.

Maps: Arapaho /Roosevelt National Forest Service Map.
Information: Arapaho/Roosevelt National Forest, Boulder Ranger District, (303) 541-2500.

Distance:	**32.0 miles round-trip**
Time:	**2 to 3 hours**
Elevation Gain:	**3730 feet**
Difficulty:	**Moderate**
Surface:	**Paved**

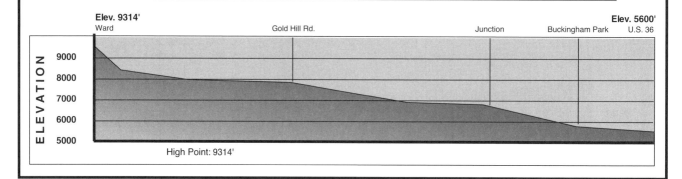

10. Meyers Gulch

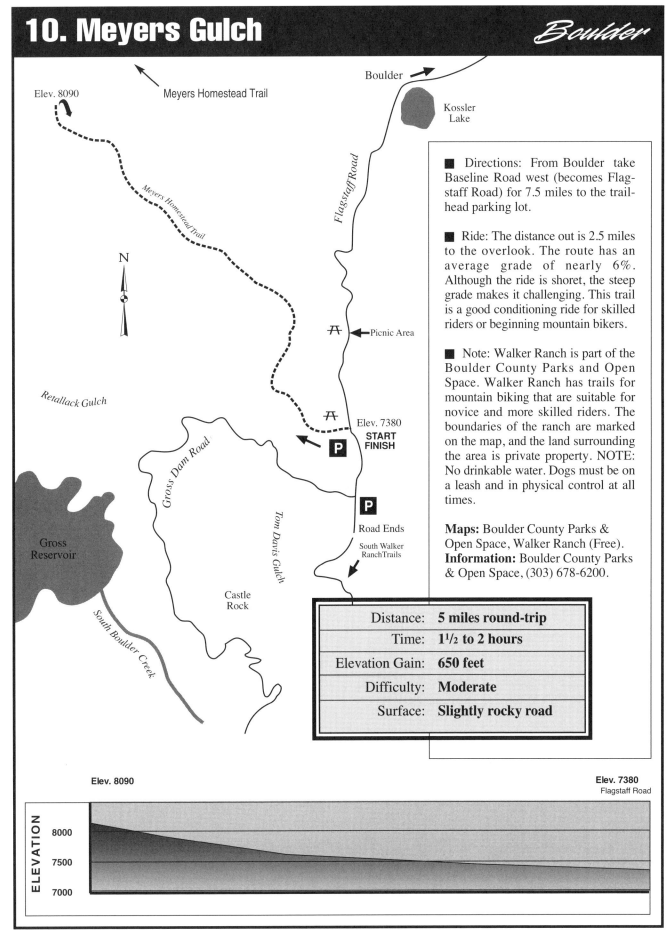

Elev. 8090

Meyers Homestead Trail

Boulder

Kossler Lake

Flagstaff Road

Meyers Homestead Trail

N

Picnic Area

Retallack Gulch

Gross Dam Road

Elev. 7380
START FINISH

P

Tom Davis Gulch

P

Road Ends

South Walker RanchTrails

Gross Reservoir

South Boulder Creek

Castle Rock

■ Directions: From Boulder take Baseline Road west (becomes Flagstaff Road) for 7.5 miles to the trailhead parking lot.

■ Ride: The distance out is 2.5 miles to the overlook. The route has an average grade of nearly 6%. Although the ride is short, the steep grade makes it challenging. This trail is a good conditioning ride for skilled riders or beginning mountain bikers.

■ Note: Walker Ranch is part of the Boulder County Parks and Open Space. Walker Ranch has trails for mountain biking that are suitable for novice and more skilled riders. The boundaries of the ranch are marked on the map, and the land surrounding the area is private property. NOTE: No drinkable water. Dogs must be on a leash and in physical control at all times.

Maps: Boulder County Parks & Open Space, Walker Ranch (Free).
Information: Boulder County Parks & Open Space, (303) 678-6200.

Distance:	**5 miles round-trip**
Time:	**1½ to 2 hours**
Elevation Gain:	**650 feet**
Difficulty:	**Moderate**
Surface:	**Slightly rocky road**

Elev. 8090

Elev. 7380
Flagstaff Road

ELEVATION

8000

7500

7000

11. Sourdough Trail

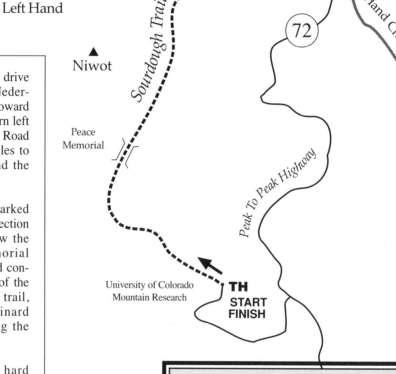

Brainard Lake Road

N

Brainard Lake

Left Hand Creek

Left Hand

Sourdough Trail

▲ Niwot

Peace Memorial

102

Ward

Left Hand Creek

72

Peak To Peak Highway

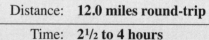

University of Colorado Mountain Research

**TH
START
FINISH**

■ Directions: From Boulder drive west on Colorado 119 to Nederland. Turn right on Hwy 72 toward Ward. Drive 7.5 miles and turn left at the C.U. Research Station Road (FS 298). Continue for 4 miles to the Sourdough trailhead and the park off road.

■ Ride: This is a well marked trail that starts with a steep section through dense pines. Follow the markers to Peace Memorial Bridge. Cross the bridge and continue up the trail to the top of the climb. From the top of the trail, descend to the paved Brainard Lake Road before returning the way you came.

■ Note: Trail surface is hard packed dirt and sometimes rocky.

Maps: USGS 7.5' Ward Quad.
Information: Arapaho/Roosevelt National Forest, Boulder Ranger District, (303) 541-2500.

Distance:	**12.0 miles round-trip**
Time:	**2½ to 4 hours**
Elevation Gain:	**1150 feet**
Difficulty:	**Moderate/Difficult**
Surface:	**Rocky but very rideable/ Single track**

Elev. 9520
Start / University Camp

Elev. 10000
Brainard Lake Drive

ELEVATION

10500

10000

9500

6.0 miles

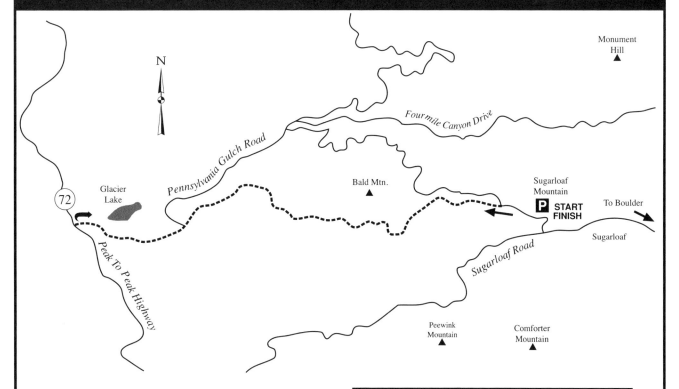

Distance:	**11.2 miles round-trip**
Time:	**1¹/₂ to 2 hours**
Elevation Gain:	**720 feet**
Difficulty:	**Easy**
Surface:	**Gravel road**

■ Directions: From Boulder travel west on Colorado 119 toward Nederland. Drive 5.4 miles and turn right on Sugarloaf Road. Travel 5 miles and turn right on Sugarloaf Mountain Road and continue for 1 mile to the trail head parking lot.

■ Ride: On the right side of the parking area there is a sign with an arrow pointing to Sunset, marking the start of the ride. The trail is marked with forest service signs at all major intersections. An old railroad bed with a 4% grades, the surface varies from smooth to rocky.

■ Notes: This trail is a gravel road that follows the old narrow gauge railroad route that served mines in the Ward/Nederland area.

Maps: USGS 7.5' Ward and Gold Hill Quads.
Information: Arapaho/Roosevelt National Forest, Boulder Ranger District, (303) 541-2500.

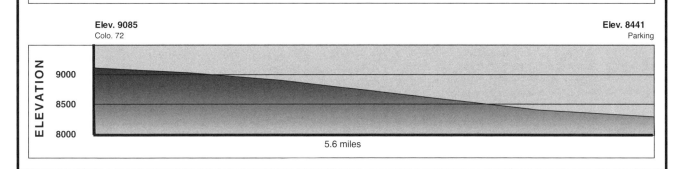

N

Jeep Trail

Miller Rock Road

▲
Miller
Rock

Cannon
Mtn.
▲

Gresham ●

Jamestown

Distance:	**7.0 miles round-trip**
Time:	**1 to 2 hours**
Elevation Gain:	**950 feet**
Difficulty:	**Moderate/Difficult**
Surface:	**Trail**

Overland Road

Overland
Mtn.
▲

← Peaceful Valley

← Ward (94) *Overland Road*

TH
START
FINISH

■ Directions: From Boulder drive 3.4 miles north on Broadway to Lee Hill Road. Turn left for 6 miles to Sunshine Canyon Road. Turn right on Lefthand Canyon. Drive for one mile, turn left and drive three miles to Jamestown. Continue for another 6.8 miles to the signed St. Vrain Trail. Turn right and park at the trailhead.

■ Ride: Start on a single track trail and follow it upstream along St. Vrain Creek. The trail ends where it intersects the creek. Turn left at the stream and climb a steep, rocky jeep road to the top of the climb. Turn left on Miller Rock Road and travel .5 mile to Miller Rock. Turn around follow the trail back to trailhead.

■ Note: In the area there are several options to this ride.

Maps: USGS 7.5' Raymond Quad.
Information: Arapaho/Roosevelt National Forest, Boulder Ranger District, (303) 541-2500.

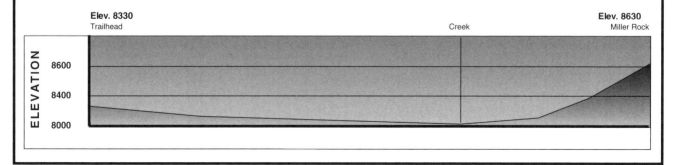

Elev. 8330
Trailhead

Creek

Elev. 8630
Miller Rock

ELEVATION

8600

8400

8000

14. Walker Ranch

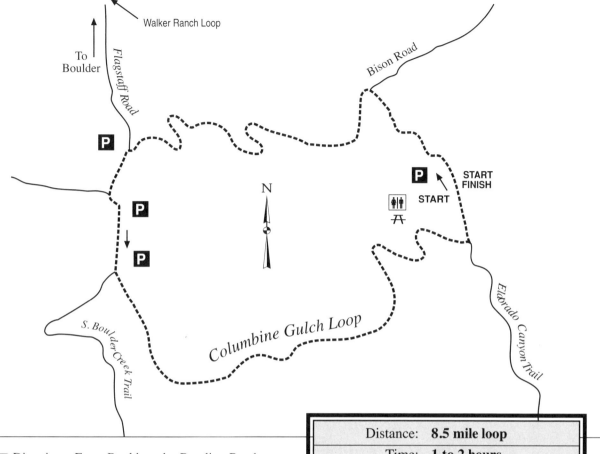

Distance:	**8.5 mile loop**
Time:	**1 to 2 hours**
Elevation Gain:	**1150 feet**
Difficulty:	**Difficult**
Surface:	**Gravel road/Trail**

■ Directions: From Boulder take Baseline Road west (becomes Flagstaff Road) for 7.5 miles. Turn east (left) on Pika Road then turn right onto Bison road and park in the Ethel Harrold Picnic Area and Trailhead parking lot.

■ Ride: From the parking lot turn left and begin the climb up Eldora Canyon Trail to Pika Road. Turn left on Pika Road and then left again onto Flagstaff Road. Turn left on Columbine Gulch Loop and descend into Eldora Canyon Trail. Then ride back to parking lot.

■ Notes: The Walker Ranch offers 2,690 acres of open space, fishing, picnic area, and seasonal restrooms. This trail is heavily used by hikers and bicyclists during weekends, so we encourage weekday use. No drinking water is available on the trail. Dogs must be on a leash at all times.

Maps: Walker Ranch Park Map (Free).
Information: Boulder County Parks & Open Space, (303) 678-6200.

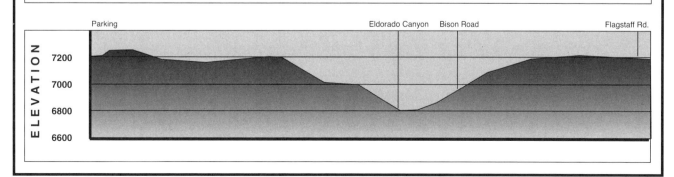

15. White Ranch

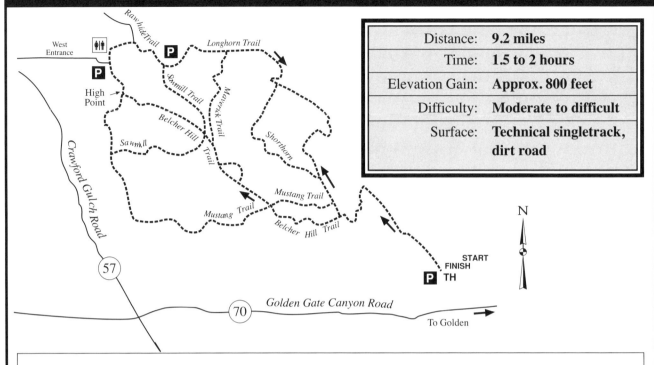

Distance:	**9.2 miles**
Time:	**1.5 to 2 hours**
Elevation Gain:	**Approx. 800 feet**
Difficulty:	**Moderate to difficult**
Surface:	**Technical singletrack, dirt road**

■ Directions: From Denver drive west on 6th Ave. (US 6) to Golden. Go north on CO 93 about 1 mile and turn left on Golden Gate Canyon Road. Turn right on Crawford Gulch Road and follow White Ranch Open Space signs to the top of White Ranch Park. Park in the main, lower parking lot.

■ Ride: From the main parking lot 0.4 mile up the road to the entrance gate, go left on Belcher Hill Trail and climb the singletrack 0.5 mile to the top of the hill. This is the highest point on White Ranch, about 8,000 feet. Stay on Belcher Hill Trail, passing a rocky crag on your right. From this vantage point you can see west across Crawford Gulch Ranch and south to Lookout Mountain. Continue down Belcher Hill 0.8 mile to Sawmill Trail,

pass on down to Maverick Trail, and turn left. After about a mile, Maverick intersects Longhorn Trail. Go left on Longhorn, at 0.3 mile veer right at the Y, and continue to Rawhide Trail. Turn right on Rawhide for a wild 0.4 mile descent. There are many water bars erected on this section so ride in control (please don't ride around the water bars). At the bottom of the hill, cross a small creek and go straight onto Wrangler's Run. Wrangler's climbs gently for half a mile. At the end of Wrangler's Run, turn left on Rawhide Trail (now a dirt service road) and ride l.l miles back to the parking lot.

Maps: White Ranch Park Map (Free).
Information: Jefferson County Open Space, (303) 271-5925.

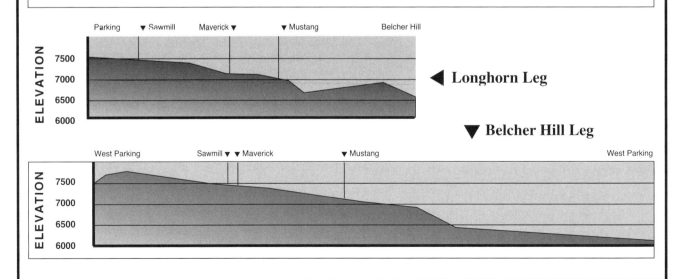

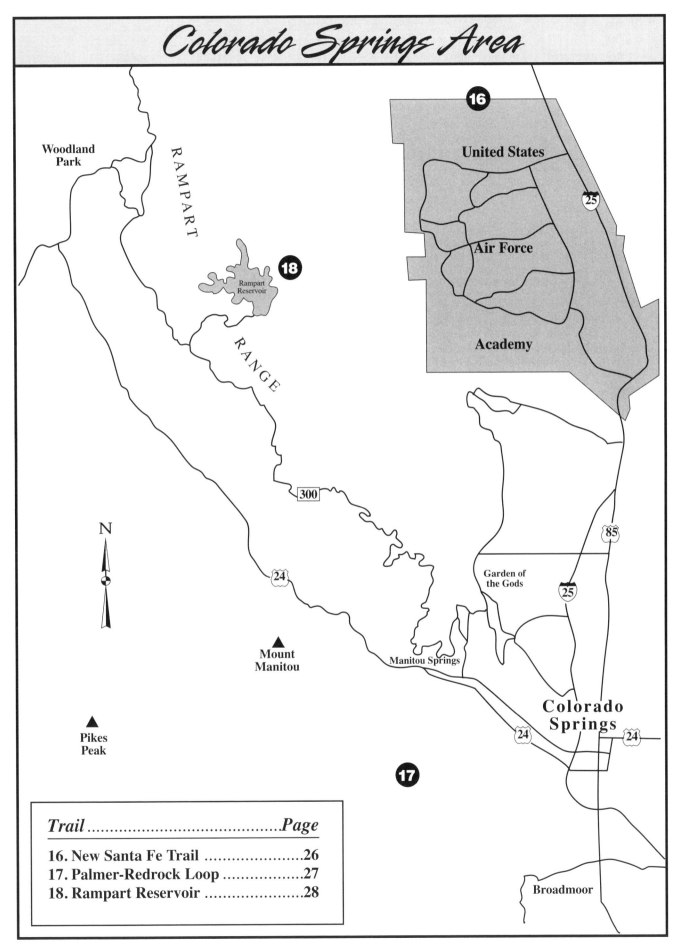

Colorado Springs Area

Woodland Park

RAMPART

Rampart Reservoir

RANGE

18

16

United States

Air Force

Academy

25

N

300

24

85

Garden of the Gods

25

Mount Manitou

Manitou Springs

Colorado Springs

24

24

Pikes Peak

17

Broadmoor

Trail	Page
16. New Santa Fe Trail	26
17. Palmer-Redrock Loop	27
18. Rampart Reservoir	28

N

START
FINISH
TH 🅿

Palmer
Lake

🛣️ 25

🛣️ 105

Monument Lake
Monument

Monument Creek

Baptist Road

North Gate Road

U.S.
Air Force
Academy

🛣️ 25

South Gate Road

Ice Lake

🅿 TH

Woodmen Road

Academy Blvd.

Colorado Springs

■ **Directions:** From Colorado Springs drive north on I-25 to the Monument / Palmer Lake exit (Highway 105). Then drive north on Colorado 105 to Palmer Lake. Drive through Palmer Lake and turn right on County Line Road. Continue 1/8 mile to the trailhead on the right.

■ **Ride:** The first 6.5 miles south from Palmer Lake are a former railroad bed. The gravel surfaced trail is straight and level. The last section is through gentle rolling hills in the Air Force Academy to the Ice Lake trailhead. The ride in the Air Force Academy section is restricted to the 6 foot wide trail.

■ **Note:** There are signs along the trail with information about the area; history, geology, geography, and the flora and fauna. The trailheads located at Palmer Lake, at Second Street in Monument, and at Baptist Road include parking areas, restrooms, and picnic tables.

Maps: New Santa Fe Trail Map (Free).
Information: El Paso County Parks, (719) 520-6375.

Distance:	**28.0 miles round-trip**
Time:	**3 to 4 hours**
Elevation Gain:	**Minimal**
Difficulty:	**Easy/Moderate**
Surface:	**Gravel Trail**

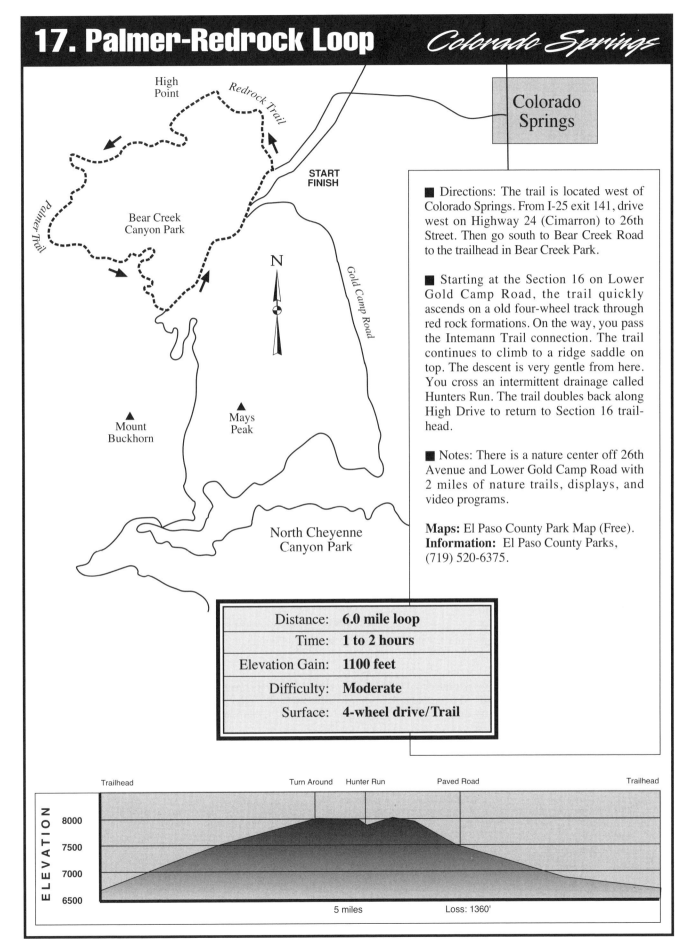

Colorado Springs

■ Directions: The trail is located west of Colorado Springs. From I-25 exit 141, drive west on Highway 24 (Cimarron) to 26th Street. Then go south to Bear Creek Road to the trailhead in Bear Creek Park.

■ Starting at the Section 16 on Lower Gold Camp Road, the trail quickly ascends on a old four-wheel track through red rock formations. On the way, you pass the Intemann Trail connection. The trail continues to climb to a ridge saddle on top. The descent is very gentle from here. You cross an intermittent drainage called Hunters Run. The trail doubles back along High Drive to return to Section 16 trailhead.

■ Notes: There is a nature center off 26th Avenue and Lower Gold Camp Road with 2 miles of nature trails, displays, and video programs.

Maps: El Paso County Park Map (Free).
Information: El Paso County Parks, (719) 520-6375.

Distance:	**6.0 mile loop**
Time:	**1 to 2 hours**
Elevation Gain:	**1100 feet**
Difficulty:	**Moderate**
Surface:	**4-wheel drive/Trail**

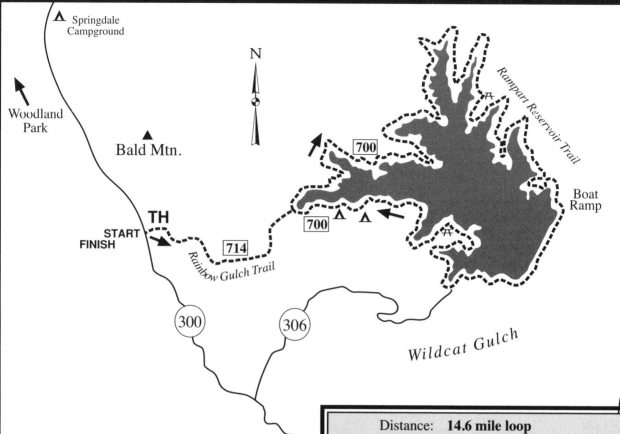

Distance: **14.6 mile loop**
Time: **2 to 4 hours**
Elevation Gain: **380 feet (TH to reservoir)**
Difficulty: **Easy**
Surface: **Native single track**

■ **Directions:** From Woodland Park take County Road 23 (Rampart Range Road) for 2.9 miles to Loy Gulch road. Turn right on Loy Gulch Road for 1.5 miles. Turn right on Rampart Range Road (FDR 300) and travel 2.2 miles. The trailhead is on the left side of the road (approximately 6.6 miles).

■ **Ride:** From the trailhead gate it's downhill to the pipeline spillway. Go left here until you reach the bridge at 1.5 miles. The trail is an 11.6 mile ride around the reservoir with several small stream crossings, and a few short sections that are technically tricky. Turn left on the Rainbow Gulch Trail #714 and return to the trailhead.

■ **Note:** Picnic facilities, restrooms and camping are available.

Maps: USGS 7.5' Cascade and Woodland Park Quads.
Information: Pike National Forest, Pikes Peak Ranger District, (719) 636-1602.

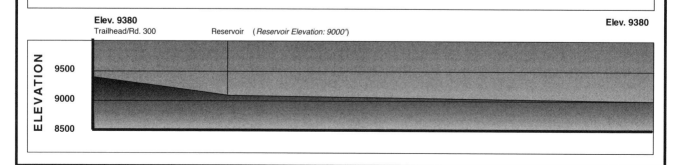

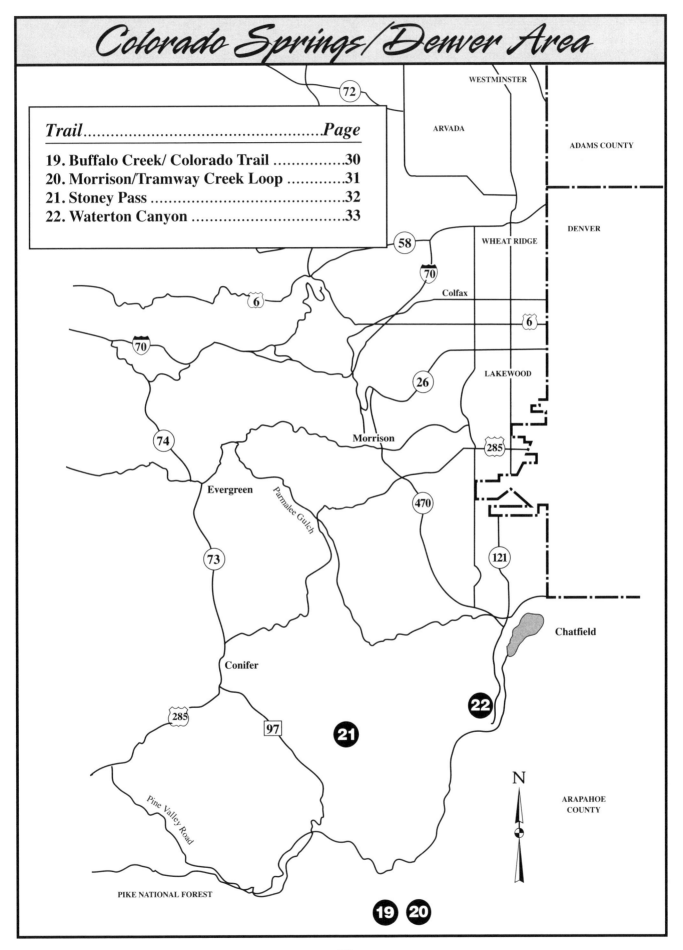

Colorado Springs/Denver Area

Trail...**Page**
19. **Buffalo Creek/ Colorado Trail** **30**
20. **Morrison/Tramway Creek Loop** **31**
21. **Stoney Pass** **32**
22. **Waterton Canyon** **33**

WESTMINSTER

ARVADA

ADAMS COUNTY

DENVER

72

58

WHEAT RIDGE

70

6

Colfax

6

70

26

LAKEWOOD

74

285

Evergreen

Parmalee Gulch

Morrison

470

73

121

Conifer

Chatfield

22

285

97

21

N

ARAPAHOE COUNTY

Pine Valley Road

PIKE NATIONAL FOREST

19 20

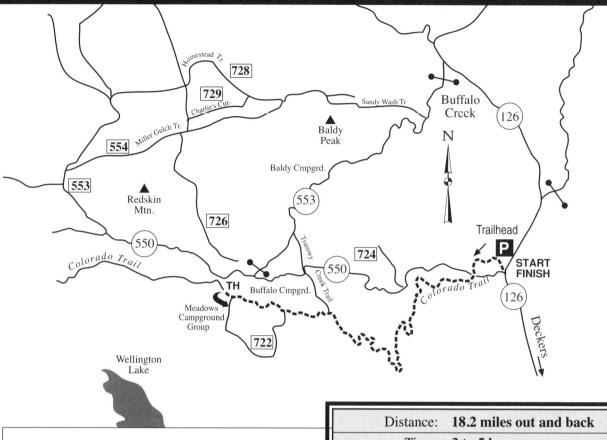

■ **Directions:** From Denver drive south on US 285 to Pine Junction, then turn left on Jefferson County Road 126 through Pine and Buffalo Creek. Continue for 3.5 miles to the Colorado Trail (1776) parking lot on the right at intersection of 126 & 550.

■ **Ride:** The trail is a classic singletrack. Go left and ride the rolls and rises, pass under large rock outcroppings (Little Scraggy Peal), cross a number of creek drainages before a gradual climb leads to where the trail joins an old logging road, which ends in a small aspen meadow. At the end of the meadow is Tramway Creek Trail. Go left, continuing on the Colorado Trail, diving down and across another (usually dry) creek bed, further to a narrow wooden bridge crossing and climb again to an open area. A newer section of singletrack rolls along and crosses an old road before the tightly curving descent to the Meadows Group Campground.

Distance:	**18.2 miles out and back**
Time:	**3 to 5 hours**
Elevation Gain:	**Approx. 2100 feet**
Difficulty:	**Moderate, but strenuous exertion level**
Surface:	**Primarily smooth single track**

Maps: Pike National Forest Map.
Information: Pike National Forest, South Platte Ranger District, (303) 275-5610.

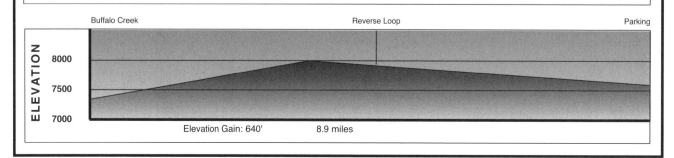

Distance: **Approx. 15 miles depending on parking**

Time: **2 to 3.5 hours**

Elevation Gain: **Approx. 1900 feet**

Difficulty: **Moderate to difficult. Exertion level high due to long climbs**

Surface: **Primarily smooth single track. 5 miles of dirt/ gravel road**

■ Directions: From Denver drive south on US 285 to Pine Junction, and take a left (south) on Jefferson County Rd 126 through Pine and Buffalo Creek. Turn right on Wellington Lake Road (FS Road 543) about 1/2 mile from Buffalo Creek. Drive up FS Road 543 about 1/2 mile and park in a turn out.

■ Ride: Go west on FS Road 543 about 2.5 miles, passing Buffalo Creek Picnic Ground and Baldy Campground. Turn left onto the Morrison Creek Trail and begin a long steady climb up the Morrison Drainage for 2 miles to Shinglemill Trail. Go right on Shinglemill which is a milder ascent on new singletrack that dips and rolls until its termination at the Colorado Trail. Go right on the Colorado Trail, and ride along the singletrack for three miles. After a long, gradual climb, the trail joins an old service road for a fast mile long descent (Watch it! There are some sandy washes, exposed roots, and a sharp pitch through a rocky creek bed.) in the Tramway Drainage. After riding through a meadow, go straight at the Tramway Creek Trail. The next 1.1 mile descent has a number of stream crossings. At FS Road 550 turn left back to FS Road 543. To get back to start, get on FS Road 543 and return to Buffalo Creek.

Maps: Pike National Forest Map.
Information: Pike National Forest, South Platte Ranger District, (303) 275-5610.

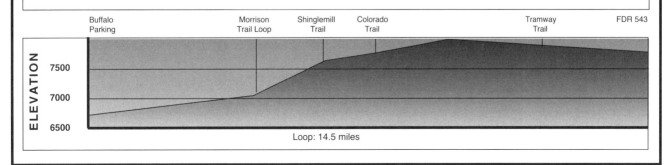

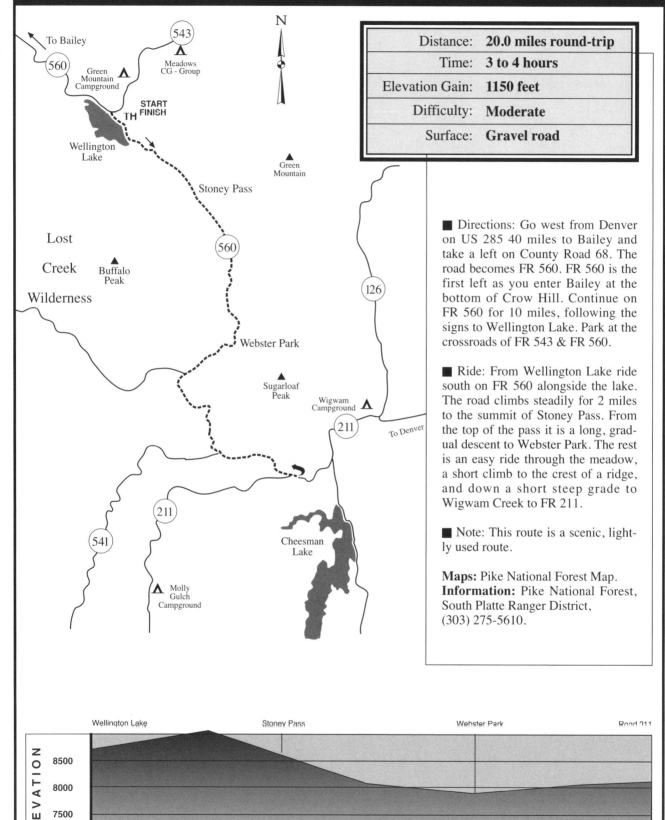

Distance:	**20.0 miles round-trip**
Time:	**3 to 4 hours**
Elevation Gain:	**1150 feet**
Difficulty:	**Moderate**
Surface:	**Gravel road**

N

To Bailey

543

560

Green Mountain Campground

Meadows CG - Group

START FINISH

TH

Wellington Lake

Green Mountain

Stoney Pass

Lost

Creek

Wilderness

560

Buffalo Peak

126

Webster Park

Sugarloaf Peak

Wigwam Campground

211

To Denver

211

541

Cheesman Lake

Molly Gulch Campground

■ Directions: Go west from Denver on US 285 40 miles to Bailey and take a left on County Road 68. The road becomes FR 560. FR 560 is the first left as you enter Bailey at the bottom of Crow Hill. Continue on FR 560 for 10 miles, following the signs to Wellington Lake. Park at the crossroads of FR 543 & FR 560.

■ Ride: From Wellington Lake ride south on FR 560 alongside the lake. The road climbs steadily for 2 miles to the summit of Stoney Pass. From the top of the pass it is a long, gradual descent to Webster Park. The rest is an easy ride through the meadow, a short climb to the crest of a ridge, and down a short steep grade to Wigwam Creek to FR 211.

■ Note: This route is a scenic, lightly used route.

Maps: Pike National Forest Map.
Information: Pike National Forest, South Platte Ranger District, (303) 275-5610.

Wellington Lake   Stoney Pass   Webster Park   Road 211

ELEVATION

8500

8000

7500

7000

10 miles one-way   Elevation Gain: 1148'

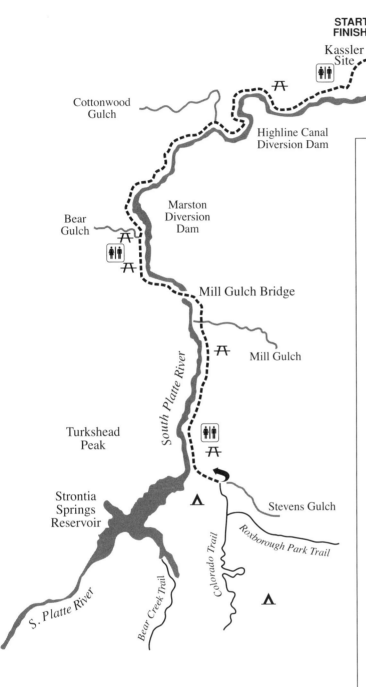

N

START FINISH TH P

Kassler Site

Platte Canyon Reservoir

Cottonwood Gulch

Highline Canal Diversion Dam

Marston Diversion Dam

Bear Gulch

Mill Gulch Bridge

Mill Gulch

South Platte River

Turkshead Peak

Strontia Springs Reservoir

Stevens Gulch

Roxborough Park Trail

Colorado Trail

Bear Creek Trail

S. Platte River

■ **Directions:** From Denver drive south on I-25 or US 85, then west on C-470 to Wadsworth Blvd. (CO 75). Drive south 4 miles to the Waterton Canyon Recreation Area. Turn left at the sign; parking area is on the right.

■ **Ride:** Ride from the Kassler Water Treatment Plant parking lot on a well maintained former railroad bed. The gentle grade makes for an enjoyable cruise up the South Platte River to the Strontia Springs Dam. Picnic tables are strategically located along the canyon so pack a lunch bag. A small herd of Bighorn sheep live in the canyon and can best be seen in the (very) early morning hours as they come down to the river. Fishing can also be good. Be aware of special regulations on some sections. From the dam you can access the East Portal of the Colorado Trial - the 456 miles cross-country trail to Durango, or a shorter loop, the Roxborough Park Trail.

■ **Notes:** Waterton Canyon is a great area for family rides, first time riders, or as a six mile warm-up for the Colorado Trail. The Waterton Canyon Recreation Area is owned by the Denver Water Board and jointly administered with the US Forest Service and Bureau of Land Management. No dogs are allowed. The canyon is extremely popular on weekends, so please, exercise responsibility and courtesy to hikers, fishermen, etc. Restrooms available at parking area and Strontia Springs Dam. Water available at parking area and at the Marston Diversion.

Maps: Pike National Forest Map.
Information: Pike National Forest, South Platte Ranger District, (303) 275-5610.

Distance:	**12.5 miles out and back**
Time:	**1.5 to 3 hours**
Elevation Gain:	**1600 feet**
Difficulty:	**Easy**
Surface:	**Maintained gravel road**

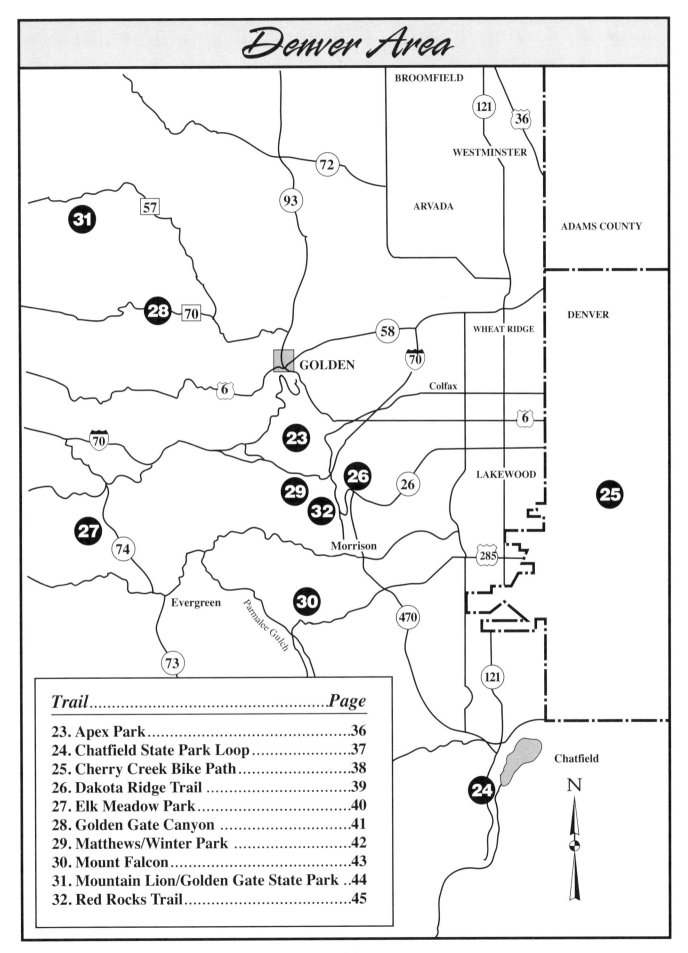

BROOMFIELD

WESTMINSTER

ARVADA

ADAMS COUNTY

DENVER

WHEAT RIDGE

GOLDEN

Colfax

LAKEWOOD

Morrison

Evergreen

Parmalee Gulch

Chatfield

N

Trail..*Page*

23. **Apex Park**...36
24. **Chatfield State Park Loop**.....................37
25. **Cherry Creek Bike Path**.......................38
26. **Dakota Ridge Trail** 39
27. **Elk Meadow Park**.................................40
28. **Golden Gate Canyon** 41
29. **Matthews/Winter Park** 42
30. **Mount Falcon**......................................43
31. **Mountain Lion/Golden Gate State Park** ..44
32. **Red Rocks Trail**..................................45

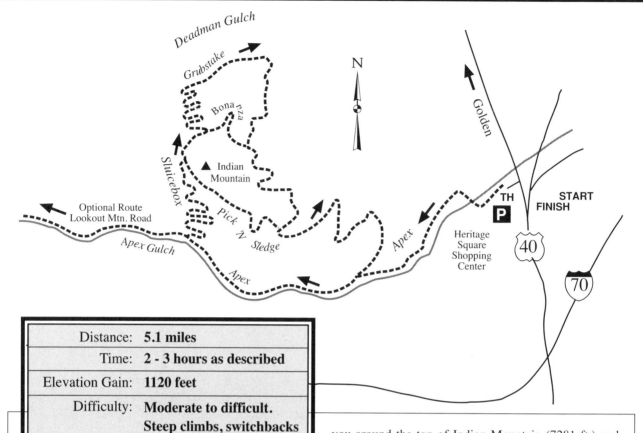

Distance:	**5.1 miles**
Time:	**2 - 3 hours as described**
Elevation Gain:	**1120 feet**
Difficulty:	**Moderate to difficult. Steep climbs, switchbacks**
Surface:	**Rocky single track**

■ **Directions:** Go west on 6th Ave (US 6) to US 40, turn left and take US 40 to Heritage Square; turn right onto Jefferson County Road 93. Go 1/4 mile and turn left at Apex Park East Access sign. (Please park in this lower lot. The upper lot is for Heritage Square patrons).

■ **Ride:** Begin by riding the new paved trail to the Apex Gulch Trail. This is a narrow rocky singletrack that was once a wagon toll road servicing the gold fields of Central City. (Optional Route: take the technically moderate 2.7 mile climb up to Lookout Mtn. Road and enjoy the fast 1.3 mile descent back to the Sluicebox Trail). Turn left and climb the switchbacks, continuing up the Grubstake Loop Trail, which brings

you around the top of Indian Mountain (7281 ft.) and back down a series of switchbacks. (A "shortcut", Bonanza Trail, cuts across the upper portion of Indian Mountain back over to Grubstake Loop). Grubstake Loop descends and rolls along Indian Mountain offering a broad panorama of the Front Range and Eastern Plains. A short climb on Grubstake and the trail intersects Pick'n'Sledge Trail. Turn left on Pick'n'Sledge for a semi-technical rocky 1 mile descent back to Apex Gulch, then left and back down to the trailhead.

■ **Notes:** Apex Park can be extremely crowded on weekends and many summer weekday evenings. Best riding times: weekdays, early mornings. No facilities.

Maps: Apex Park Map (Free).
Information: Jefferson County Open Space, (303) 271-5925.

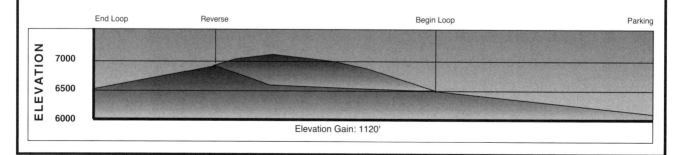

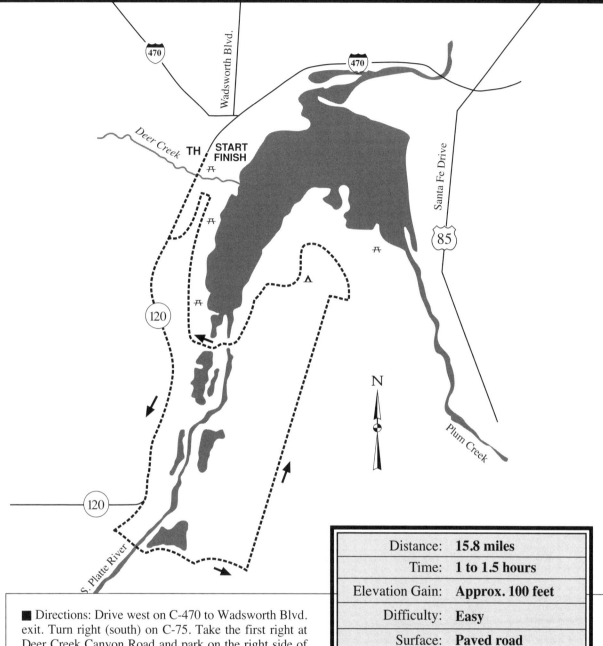

Distance:	**15.8 miles**
Time:	**1 to 1.5 hours**
Elevation Gain:	**Approx. 100 feet**
Difficulty:	**Easy**
Surface:	**Paved road**

■ Directions: Drive west on C-470 to Wadsworth Blvd. exit. Turn right (south) on C-75. Take the first right at Deer Creek Canyon Road and park on the right side of the road (across from the Chatfield Arboretum).

■ Ride: Ride south on C-75, 4.3 miles to Kassler Road (signs also point out Waterton Canyon/ Roxborough Park), then turn left and ride past the water treatment plant. Cross the South Platte River and continue riding to Rampart Road. Turn left and ride the rolling hills to Titan Road, then go right on Titan Road a short way turning left on Roxborough Park Road. Pass through the East entrance gate of Chatfield Recreation Area and follow the road around the back side of the reservoir, through the west gate, right on C-75 and back to the parking area.

■ Notes: A very popular training ride with Denver area cyclists, this loop has little elevation gain with a few rolling hills. The terrain is diverse enough to keep you entertained. Inside Chatfield Recreation Area keep an eye out for waterfowl ranging from geese and ducks to loons and Great Blue Herons. Restrooms and water available in Chatfield Recreation Area.

Information: Chatfield State Park, (303) 791-7275.

Downtown Denver

Confluence Park

START FINISH

15th Street

Broadway

Auraria Campus

City Park

Speer Boulevard

Cherry Creek

Downing Street

East Colfax Avenue

25

First Ave.

Cherry Creek Shopping Center

N

Denver Country Club

University Blvd.

Colorado Blvd.

Washington Park

Distance:	**10.0 miles round-trip**
Time:	**1 to 2 hours**
Elevation Gain:	**Minimal**
Difficulty:	**Easy**
Surface:	**Paved**

■ Directions: Confluence Park is located in Denver at the confluence of the Platte River and Cherry Creek. The park is on the west side of the 15th Street underpass near lower downtown Denver (at 15th Street and Little Raven Street).

■ Ride: A smooth easy ride on a wide paved path through the heart of Denver from Confluence Park to the Cherry Creek Shopping Center. The path is below street level alongside Cherry Creek from Confluence Park to 1st & Lafayette. Exit ramps provide access to Auraria campus, downtown Denver, and farther east,

Washington Park. At 1st & Lafayette you exit to a wide sidewalk on 1st Avenue. Pass the Denver Country Club and ride east to the Cherry Creek Shopping Center. This is a relaxing ride that the entire family can take through the heart of Denver without automobile traffic.

■ Note: Exit and entrance ramps are approximately two blocks apart.

Maps: Denver City Map.
Information: City & County of Denver Parks and Recreation Department, (720) 913-0741.

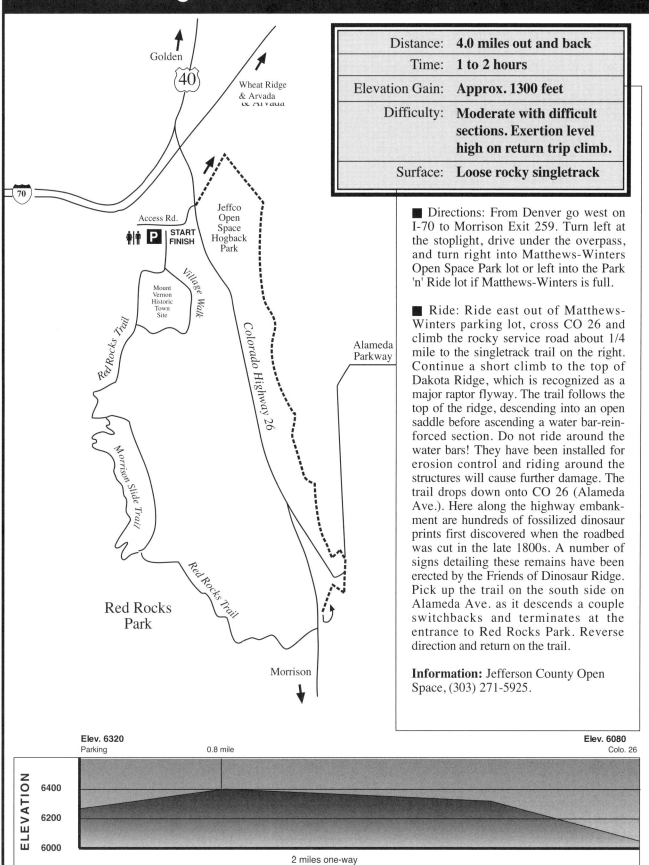

Distance:	**4.0 miles out and back**
Time:	**1 to 2 hours**
Elevation Gain:	**Approx. 1300 feet**
Difficulty:	**Moderate with difficult sections. Exertion level high on return trip climb.**
Surface:	**Loose rocky singletrack**

■ Directions: From Denver go west on I-70 to Morrison Exit 259. Turn left at the stoplight, drive under the overpass, and turn right into Matthews-Winters Open Space Park lot or left into the Park 'n' Ride lot if Matthews-Winters is full.

■ Ride: Ride east out of Matthews-Winters parking lot, cross CO 26 and climb the rocky service road about 1/4 mile to the singletrack trail on the right. Continue a short climb to the top of Dakota Ridge, which is recognized as a major raptor flyway. The trail follows the top of the ridge, descending into an open saddle before ascending a water bar-reinforced section. Do not ride around the water bars! They have been installed for erosion control and riding around the structures will cause further damage. The trail drops down onto CO 26 (Alameda Ave.). Here along the highway embankment are hundreds of fossilized dinosaur prints first discovered when the roadbed was cut in the late 1800s. A number of signs detailing these remains have been erected by the Friends of Dinosaur Ridge. Pick up the trail on the south side on Alameda Ave. as it descends a couple switchbacks and terminates at the entrance to Red Rocks Park. Reverse direction and return on the trail.

Information: Jefferson County Open Space, (303) 271-5925.

■ **Directions:** From Denver drive west on I-70 to Evergreen Parkway (formally El Rancho) exit 252, through Bergen Park. Continue on CO 74 about 3/4 mile; Elk Meadow Open Space Park parking lot is on the right.

■ **Ride:** From the parking lot ride south on Painter's Pause Trail, a smooth 1 mile descent through a big meadow, turning right onto Sleepy "S" Trail. Stay on Sleepy "S" for 1.1 miles as it winds and gently climbs to the Meadow View Trail. Go right on Meadow View for 1.6 miles as it climbs a couple switchbacks and traverses wooded hillsides overlooking the Wildlife Preserve. Stay on Meadow View Trail for another 0.9 mile back to the parking area. This lower loop of Elk Meadow Park is excellent for mixed rider abilities, not extremely challenging, with smooth single track and a couple of switchbacks and water bars. Gonzos can tackle the upper trails - Bergen Peak and Too Long Trail - for a strenuous technical ride.

Maps: Elk Meadow Park Map (Free).
Information: Jefferson County Open Space, (303) 271-5925

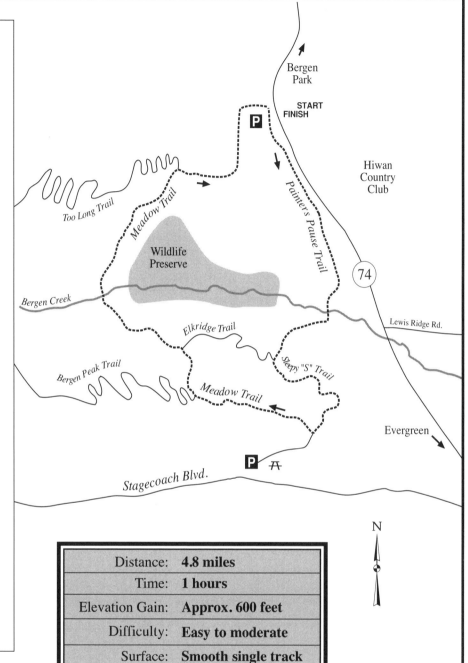

Distance:	**4.8 miles**
Time:	**1 hours**
Elevation Gain:	**Approx. 600 feet**
Difficulty:	**Easy to moderate**
Surface:	**Smooth single track**

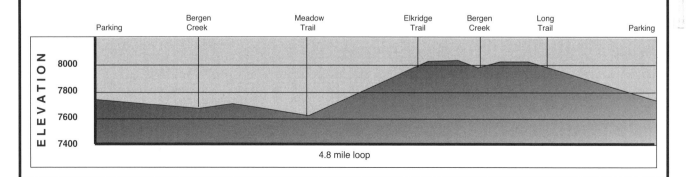

28. Golden Gate Canyon

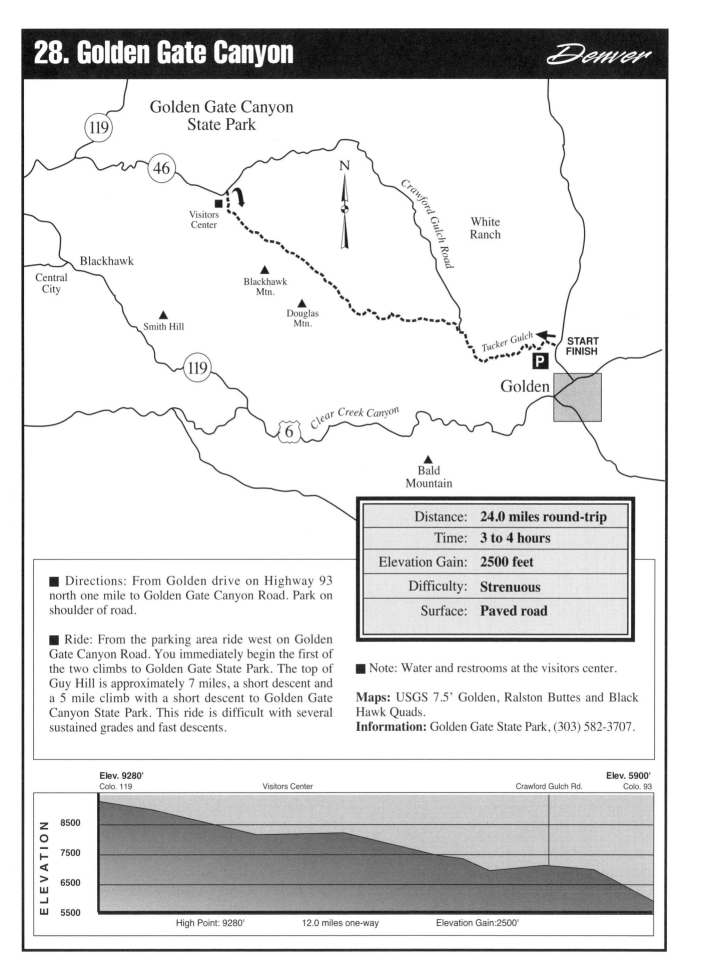

Golden Gate Canyon State Park

Distance:	**24.0 miles round-trip**
Time:	**3 to 4 hours**
Elevation Gain:	**2500 feet**
Difficulty:	**Strenuous**
Surface:	**Paved road**

■ Directions: From Golden drive on Highway 93 north one mile to Golden Gate Canyon Road. Park on shoulder of road.

■ Ride: From the parking area ride west on Golden Gate Canyon Road. You immediately begin the first of the two climbs to Golden Gate State Park. The top of Guy Hill is approximately 7 miles, a short descent and a 5 mile climb with a short descent to Golden Gate Canyon State Park. This ride is difficult with several sustained grades and fast descents.

■ Note: Water and restrooms at the visitors center.

Maps: USGS 7.5' Golden, Ralston Buttes and Black Hawk Quads.
Information: Golden Gate State Park, (303) 582-3707.

Denver

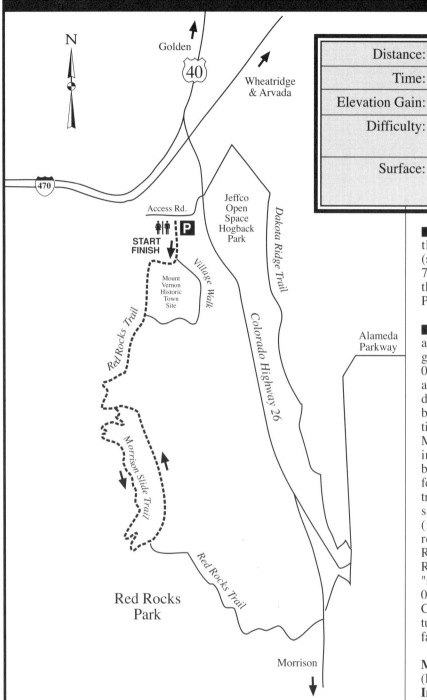

N

Golden

40

Wheatridge & Arvada

470

Access Rd.

Jeffco Open Space Hogback Park

Dakota Ridge Trail

START FINISH

P

Village Walk

Mount Vernon Historic Town Site

Red Rocks Trail

Colorado Highway 26

Alameda Parkway

Morrison Slide Trail

Red Rocks Park

Red Rocks Trail

Morrison

Distance:	**5.1 miles**
Time:	**1 to 1.5 hours**
Elevation Gain:	**500 feet**
Difficulty:	**Easy to moderate. One difficult descent.**
Surface:	**Mostly smooth single track. Rocky switchbacks.**

■ Directions: Drive west on I-70 to the Morrison exit #259. Turn left (south) at the stoplight, drive under I-70 about 1/4 mile, and turn right into the Matthews/ Winters Open Space Park parking lot.

■ Ride: Through the picnic area, cross a wooden bridge, veer right and begin a gentle climb up Village Walk Trail. At 0.5 miles go right on Red Rocks Trail, a smooth singletrack that curves and dips for 0.7 mile into Cherry Gulch before briefly climbing to the intersection with Morrison Slide Trail. Ride up Morrison Slide for 1.2 miles, negotiating the moderately difficult switchbacks until you top the mesa at 6,800 feet. The back side of Morrison Slide is tricky - loose rocks, a number of tight switchbacks with steep drop-offs (remember your helmet!) - but a rewarding descent back to the Red Rocks Trail intersection. Go straight on Red Rocks Trail as it climbs up a short "slickrock" section and rolls along for 0.8 mile. Continue back down through Cherry Gulch on Red Rocks Trail, then turn right on Village Walk Trail for the fast 0.6 mile cruise to the parking lot.

Maps: Matthews/Winters Park Maps, (Free).
Information: Jefferson County Open Space, (303) 271-5925.

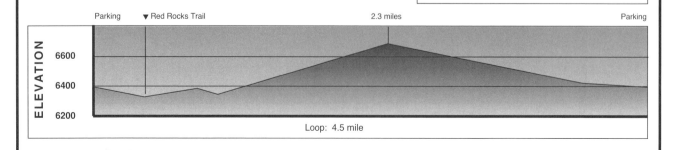

Parking   ▼ Red Rocks Trail   2.3 miles   Parking

ELEVATION

6600

6400

6200

Loop: 4.5 mile

30. Mount Falcon

Distance:	**4.2 miles**
Time:	**2 to 3 hours as described**
Elevation Gain:	**1900 feet**
Difficulty:	**Moderate. Exertion high**
Surface:	**Service road, singletrack**

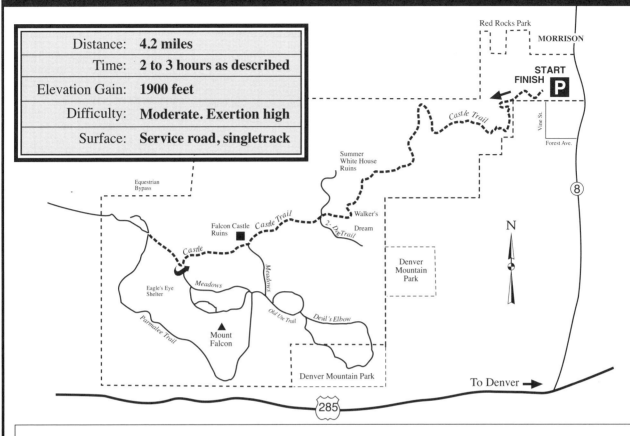

■ Directions: Drive south from Denver on US 285 to CO 8. Go about 1 mile to Forest Ave, turn left and follow the brown Open Space signs to Mt. Falcon Park.

■ The Castle Trail begins at the Morrison Trailhead as a rocky singletrack that goes through a dry wash and climbs to an old service road. Walker's Dream Shelter is at the top of the 2.7 mile climb and offers a nice view of Denver. A quick tour of the Summer White House ruins is accessed by a .3 mile trail on the right. The Castle trail continues as a flat service road for 1.2 miles to the upper parking lot. At the parking lot you can top off your water bottles at the pump. Turn around at this point and return on the Castle Trail for a fun fast descent (7.8 miles total). Or for singletrack challenge, take the Parmalee Trail, which descends into Parmalee Gulch and climbs steeply back up to the Meadow Trail. Go right on Meadow Trail and ride straight onto Old Ute trail, a short climb with more good views. Stay on Old Ute Trail at Devil's Elbow (unless you like extremely steep challenges); go back to Meadow Trail and turn right again for a quick 0.3 mile roll across the meadow and back to Castle Trail. Turn right and descend to the parking lot. (Watch your speed! This fast descent is your reward for all that climbing, but it can get a little sketchy with loose rocks and water bars. Give right-of-way to all uphill traffic).

Maps: Mount Falcon Map, (Free).
Information: Jefferson County Open Space, (303) 271-5925

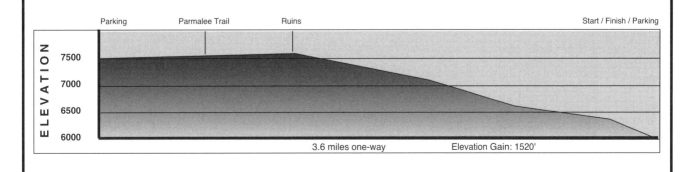

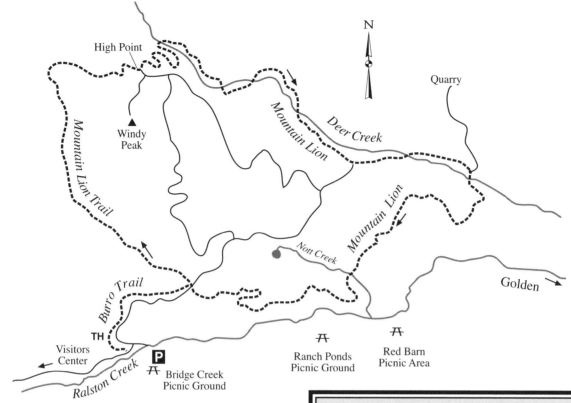

Distance:	**7.0 mile loop**
Time:	**2 to 3 hours**
Elevation Gain:	**1720 feet**
Difficulty:	**Moderate/Difficult**
Surface:	**Gravel road/ Single track**

■ **Directions:** From Golden, go north on Highway 93 one mile to Golden Gate Canyon Road, then west for 12 miles to the Visitors Center (Parks pass required). Turn right and travel 1¾ miles on Ralston Creek Road to the Bridge Creek Parking Area.

■ **Ride:** From Bridge Creek it is a gradual grade up Burro Trail to Mountain Lion Trail; stay left. It is a steady climb to the high point. Once at the top, ride down a short series of switchbacks to Deer Creek. Along Deer Creek, ride through a series of stream crossings, and continue on Mountain Lion Trail back to the parking area. Rocks, roots and creeks encountered on the ride require some technical skills.

■ **Notes:** There are a number of well marked trails in the park for riders of all skill levels.

Maps: Golden Gate Canyon State Park Trail Map, (Free).
Information: Golden Gate State Park, (303) 582-3707.

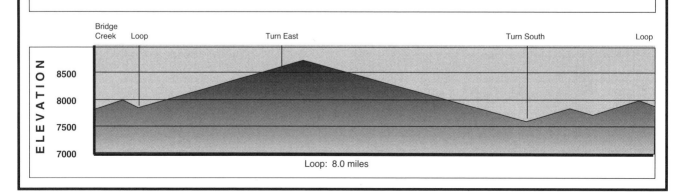

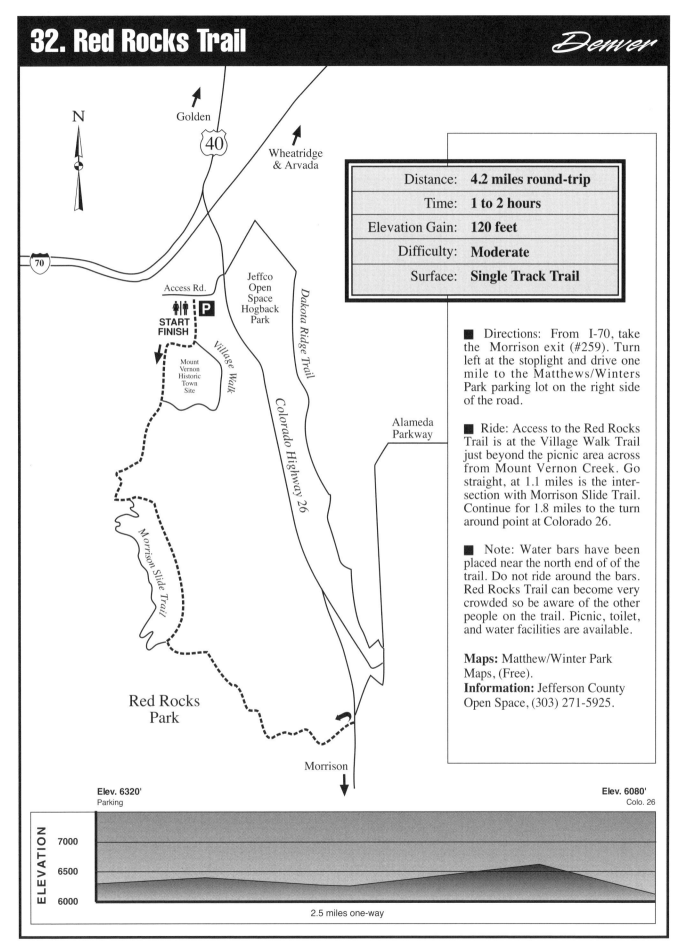

N

Golden

40

Wheatridge & Arvada

70

Access Rd.

START FINISH

P

Jeffco Open Space Hogback Park

Dakota Ridge Trail

Mount Vernon Historic Town Site

Village Walk

Colorado Highway 26

Alameda Parkway

Morrison Slide Trail

Red Rocks Park

Morrison

Distance:	**4.2 miles round-trip**
Time:	**1 to 2 hours**
Elevation Gain:	**120 feet**
Difficulty:	**Moderate**
Surface:	**Single Track Trail**

■ Directions: From I-70, take the Morrison exit (#259). Turn left at the stoplight and drive one mile to the Matthews/Winters Park parking lot on the right side of the road.

■ Ride: Access to the Red Rocks Trail is at the Village Walk Trail just beyond the picnic area across from Mount Vernon Creek. Go straight, at 1.1 miles is the intersection with Morrison Slide Trail. Continue for 1.8 miles to the turn around point at Colorado 26.

■ Note: Water bars have been placed near the north end of of the trail. Do not ride around the bars. Red Rocks Trail can become very crowded so be aware of the other people on the trail. Picnic, toilet, and water facilities are available.

Maps: Matthew/Winter Park Maps, (Free).
Information: Jefferson County Open Space, (303) 271-5925.

Elev. 6320'
Parking

Elev. 6080'
Colo. 26

ELEVATION

7000

6500

6000

2.5 miles one-way

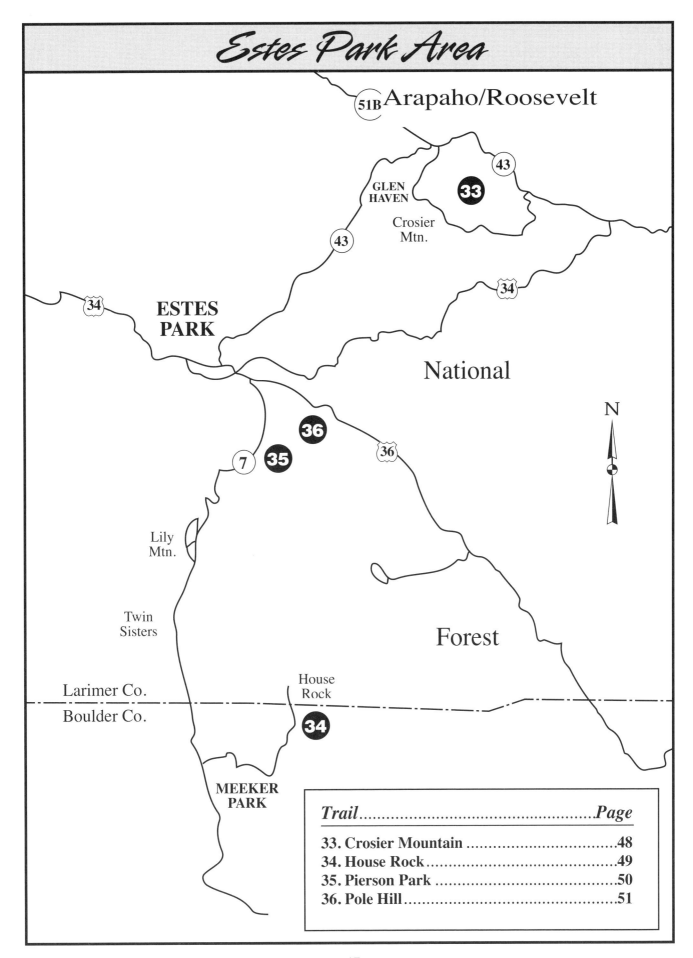

Estes Park Area

51B Arapaho/Roosevelt

43

33

GLEN
HAVEN

Crosier
Mtn.

43

34

National

ESTES
PARK

34

N

36

7   35   36

Lily
Mtn.

Twin
Sisters

Forest

Larimer Co.

House
Rock

Boulder Co.

34

MEEKER
PARK

Trail	Page
33. Crosier Mountain	48
34. House Rock	49
35. Pierson Park	50
36. Pole Hill	51

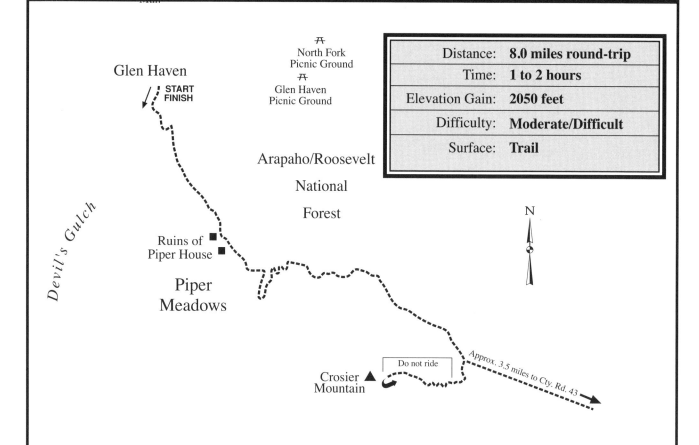

Glen Haven

START
FINISH

North Fork
Picnic Ground

Glen Haven
Picnic Ground

Arapaho/Roosevelt

National

Forest

Devil's Gulch

Ruins of
Piper House

Piper
Meadows

N

Crosier ▲
Mountain

Do not ride

Approx. 3.5 miles to Cty. Rd. 43

Distance:	**8.0 miles round-trip**
Time:	**1 to 2 hours**
Elevation Gain:	**2050 feet**
Difficulty:	**Moderate/Difficult**
Surface:	**Trail**

■ Directions: From Estes Park take the Devils Gulch Road (County Road 43) to Glen Haven. Just south of Glen Haven at the livery stables, there is a dirt road going south marked by a Crosier Mountain Trail sign. Park your vehicle off the road.

■ Ride: From Devils Gulch Road follow the Forest Service sign Crosier Mountain Trail. Follow the trail over a gully and up through a series of switchbacks. Keep to the left as you ride uphill. At Piper Meadow stay left at the branch in the trail, along the east edge of the meadow. Ride south to the end of the meadow to a Forest Service sign, then ride up a draw, making a

series of switchbacks to ridge. The trail climbs through valleys and ridges to the 1/2 mile sign to Crosier Mountain. Because of erosion problems, park your bike at the sign and walk to the peak. It is a continuous climb from the trailhead to Crosier Mountain.

■ Notes: Carry water, because none is available along the way.

Maps: USGS 7.5' Glen Haven Quad, Arapaho/ Roosevelt Forest Map.
Information: Forest Service Visitors Center, Summer (970) 586-3440, Winter (970) 295-6700.

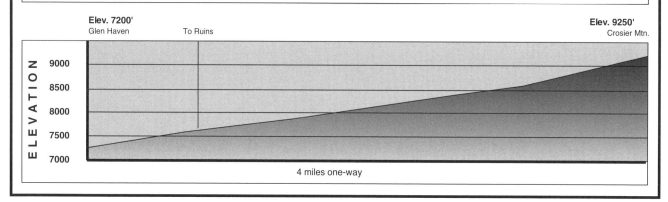

Elev. 7200'
Glen Haven

To Ruins

Elev. 9250'
Crosier Mtn.

ELEVATION: 9000, 8500, 8000, 7500, 7000

4 miles one-way

■ **Directions:** Go 8 miles south of Estes Park on Colorado Hwy 7 to Meeker Park; park at the campground.

■ **Ride:** Ride south on Colorado 7 to Cabin Creek Road. Turn left on the gravel road. Passing through a residential area, continue to an unmarked intersection where you turn right along Cabin Creek. Ride 3 miles to the sign for House Rock and turn left onto the Park Road. From this point the route gets tougher; it is a continuous climb from here. The elevation gain is 780 feet in 3 miles. It is a four-wheel drive road with ruts and loose gravel to House Rock.

■ **Notes:** Scenic ride that requires some technical riding skills.

Maps: USGS 7.5' Allen's Park, Raymond, Panorama Peak Quads, Arapaho/ Roosevelt National Forest.
Information: Forest Service Visitors Center, Summer (970) 586-3440, Winter (970) 295-6700.

To Estes Park

N

House Rock

Big Owl Road

Pierson Park Road

⑦

Camp St. Malo

Mount Meeker Campground ▲

Cabin Creek Road

START FINISH

Meeker Park

Copeland Moraine

Deer Ridge

Distance:	**9.0 miles round-trip**
Time:	**3 to 4 hours**
Elevation Gain:	**780 feet**
Difficulty:	**Difficult**
Surface:	**Gravel road**

Elev. 8500'
Meeker Park

Pierson Park Rd.

Elev. 9280'
House Rock Turnaround

ELEVATION

9500
9000
8500
8000

4.5 miles one-way   Elevation Gain: 780'

Estes Park

■ Directions: From Estes Park follow Highway 7 south to Meeker Park and turn east onto County Road 82. Follow County Road 82 to FR 119 (Pierson Park Road).

■ Ride: Pierson Park Road runs north and south along the valleys below and east of Twin Sisters Peaks. The road heads to the north ascending and descending several steep hills. Numerous, numbered open side routes lead off to the West. Eventually the road connects to the subdivision in Little Valley. Follow the subdivision roads down to the paved Fish Creek Road, and travel north to Estes Park. It is 10 miles back to Estes Park via Pierson Park on the Pierson Park Road.

Maps: USGS 7.5' Panorama Peak, Raymond Quads.
Information: Arapaho/ Roosevelt National Forest, Canyon Lakes Ranger District, (970) 295-6700.

Distance:	**20 miles round-trip**
Time:	**4 to 6 hours**
Elevation Gain:	**1000 feet**
Difficulty:	**Moderate**
Surface:	**Double Tread Trail**

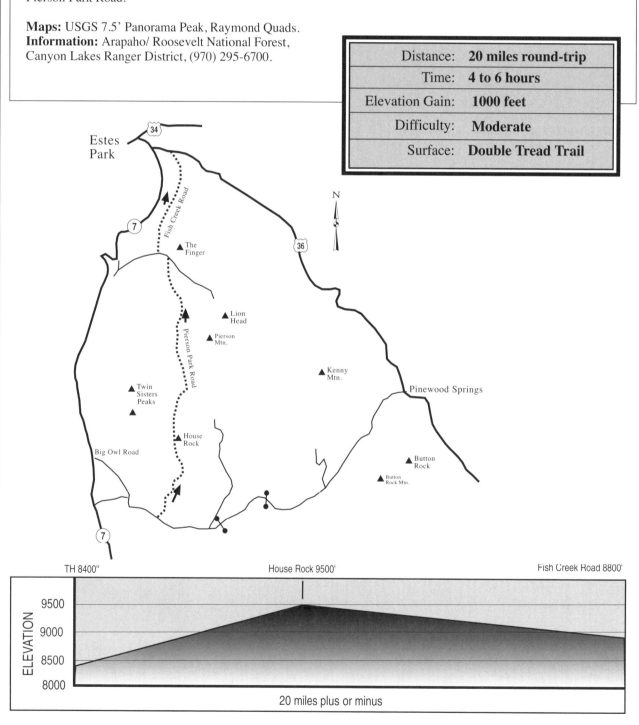

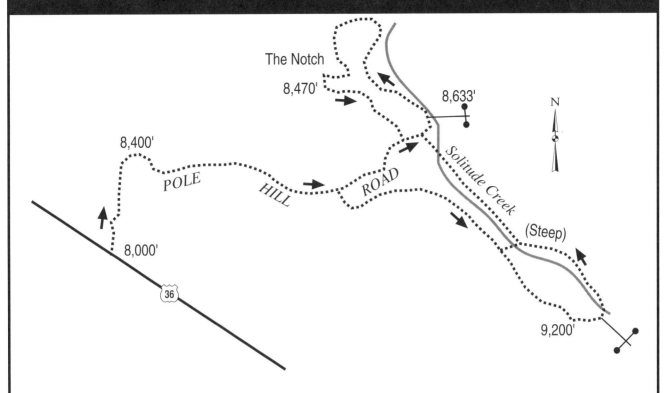

Directions: From Estes Park travel 3 miles east on Hwy 36 to the top of Park Hill. This entrance puts you on the dirt road signed as Pole Hill Road.

Ride: Pole Hill provides a couple of loop options with a variety of views and terrains. The Notch Loop is located 1.5 miles from the Forest boundary and travels north of the main road. The observation platform at the notch is an excellent point for viewing the Estes Valley, the Mummy Range to the north, Flatop Mountain and Hallet Peak west along the Continental Divide.

Continuing on the road past the observation platform you will descend to Solitude Creek. This north-south canyon receives very little light which makes it a cooler, moister place than the surrounding area.

Pole Hill Road starts on private land with many side roads branching off. The National Forest boundary is .9 mile from the highway and is marked by a forest welcome sign. There is no designated parking lot on the Pole Hill road so parking is limited to the roadside. Please keep the roadways clear.

Maps: 7.5' Panorama Peak Quad.
Information: Arapaho/Roosevelt National Forest, Canyon Lakes Ranger District, (970) 295-6700.

Distance:	**10 mile loop**
Time:	**4 to 6 hours**
Elevation Gain:	**1200 feet**
Difficulty:	**Moderate**
Surface:	**Double Tread Trail**

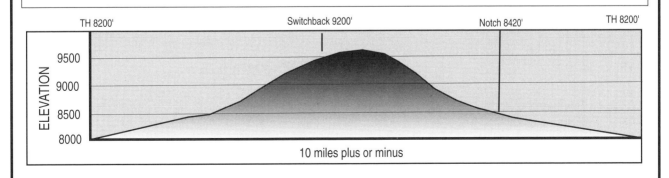

Fort Collins Area

Trail	Page
37. Foothills Trail	54
38. Hewlett Gulch	55
39. Horsetooth Rock Trail	56
40. Red Feather Lakes Loop	57

40 RED FEATHER LAKES

74E

38

285

POUDRE PARK

14

Cache La Poudre Wilderness

Wilderness

Arapaho/Roosevelt

National

Forest

N

37

Lory State Park

FORT COLLINS

Horsetooth Reservoir

Wilderness

39

Rocky Mtn. Nat'l. Park

38E

EXPLORE THE CANYON LAKES RANGER DISTRICT ON MOUNTAIN BIKES

Canyon Lakes Ranger District of the Arapaho and Roosevelt National Forest is located approximately 50 miles northwest of Fort Collins, Colorado. Within the Canyon Lakes District are 168 miles of roads and trails for mountain bike enthusiasts of all ages and abilities to test their skills and to enjoy the scenery of their National Forest. These routes traverse the foothills of the Front Range and the Colorado high country. They wander through meadows and forests and along streams and rivers. They offer mountain bikers a chance to explore the natural beauty of an area, to view wildlife and to get away and experience the wonder of the Arapaho/Roosevelt National Forest.

Located throughout the Canyon Lakes District are camping areas. These provide a place for mountain bikers to rest and recap the day's new discoveries and to plan for tomorrow's new adventures. The village of Red Feather Lakes is a small mountain community, located within the Arapaho/Roosevelt National Forest, that provides mountain bikers with basic supplies. There are no bike shops in Red Feather Lakes. The closest area with bike supplies, repairs and rentals is Fort Collins.

For additional information on mountain biking on the Canyon Lakes Ranger District call (970) 295-6700.

■ **Directions:** The trail is west of Fort Collins and on the east side Horsetooth Reservoir and begins at Pineridge Open Space Park.

■ **Ride:** From the parking area near Dixon Reservoir ride north along the west side of Dixon Reservoir. Cross the road (CR 42C), to the trail left of the irrigation ditch. Ride the main trail for approximately one mile to the start of a short climb up a series of tricky switchbacks. At the top of the ridge, the trail parallels Centennial Drive. You will cross the road twice before nearing College Lake. Near Soldier Dam the trail drops down the ridge. Go left at a trail junction and climb the ridge to the Campeau parking area. If you go right, it's about 3/4 of a mile to Michaud Lane. The two steep grades can necessitate walking your bike.

■ **Notes:** Bicyclists must yield to foot and horse traffic.

Maps: USGS 7.5' Horsetooth Reservoir Quad, Open Space Trails Guide, (Free).
Information: Fort Collins Parks & Open Land Department, (970) 221-6660.

Distance:	**10.0 miles round-trip**
Time:	**2 to 3 hours**
Elevation Gain:	**300 feet**
Difficulty:	**Moderate/Difficult**
Surface:	**Dirt trail**

Map labels: Michaud Lane, Horsetooth Dam, Soldier Canyon Dam, Lory State Park, College Lake, High Point, Overland Trail, Fort Collins, Horsetooth Mountain Park, Horsetooth Mountain, Spring Canyon, START FINISH, Dixon Reservoir, 23N, Spring Canyon Dam, Dry Lake, N

Elevation profile: Elev. 5280' Start, Dixon Dam, Filtration Plant, Elev. 5540' Michaud Lane; 5.0 miles; Elevation Gain: 300'

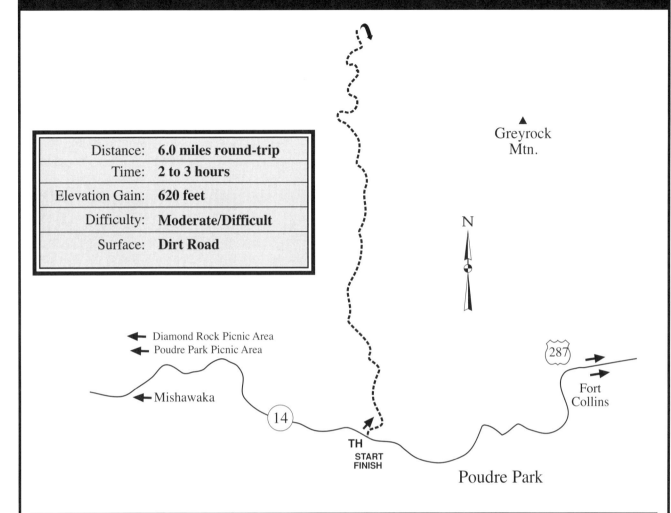

Distance:	**6.0 miles round-trip**
Time:	**2 to 3 hours**
Elevation Gain:	**620 feet**
Difficulty:	**Moderate/Difficult**
Surface:	**Dirt Road**

Greyrock Mtn.

Diamond Rock Picnic Area
Poudre Park Picnic Area

Mishawaka

14

287

Fort Collins

TH
START
FINISH

Poudre Park

■ Directions: From Fort Collins drive west on Highway 14 to Poudre Park. A short distance past the town on your right there is a bridge over the Cache la Poudre River to Hewlett Gulch. Past the bridge is a parking area on the right.

■ Ride: Cross the bridge and follow the road straight ahead, following Gorden Creek up the trail. This is a good trail with some rocky sections and numerous stream crossings. The ride is a steady climb with a few

steep sections but generally easy. Prepare to occasionally wade the stream.

■ Notes: The bridge has a gate but it is open to the public. No drinking water available.

Maps: USGS 7.5' Poudre Park Quad, Arapaho/ Roosevelt National Forest Map.
Information: Arapaho/Roosevelt National Forest, Canyon Lakes Ranger District, (970) 295-6700.

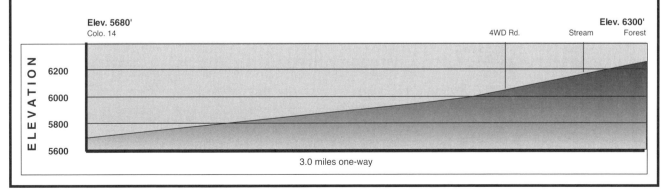

Elev. 5680'
Colo. 14

4WD Rd. Stream **Elev. 6300'** Forest

ELEVATION

6200
6000
5800
5600

3.0 miles one-way

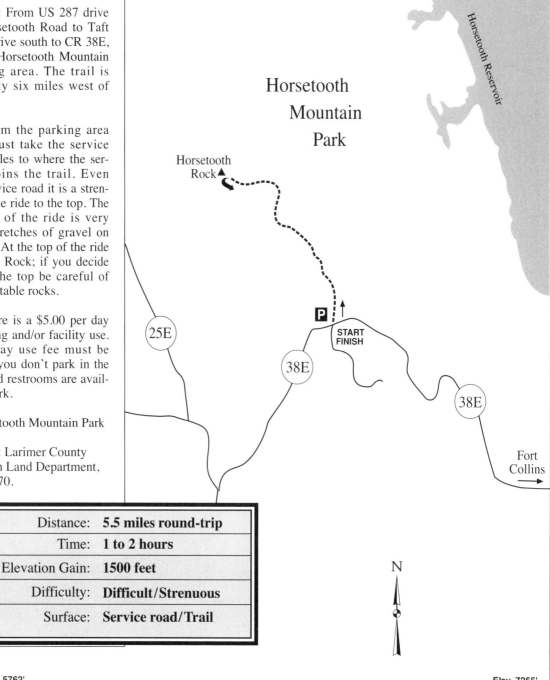

■ **Directions:** From US 287 drive west on Horsetooth Road to Taft Hill Road. Drive south to CR 38E, and west to Horsetooth Mountain Park parking area. The trail is approximately six miles west of Fort Collins.

■ **Ride:** From the parking area bicyclists must take the service road up 2 miles to where the service road joins the trail. Even using the service road it is a strenuous 2.75 mile ride to the top. The trail portion of the ride is very steep with stretches of gravel on smooth rock. At the top of the ride is Horsetooth Rock; if you decide to climb to the top be careful of loose and unstable rocks.

■ **Note:** There is a $5.00 per day fee for parking and/or facility use. The $5.00 day use fee must be paid even if you don't park in the lot. Water and restrooms are available in the park.

Maps: Horsetooth Mountain Park Map, (Free).
Information: Larimer County Parks & Open Land Department, (970) 679-4570.

Horsetooth Mountain Park

Horsetooth Rock▲

Horsetooth Reservoir

25E

P
START FINISH

38E

38E

Fort Collins

N

Distance:	**5.5 miles round-trip**
Time:	**1 to 2 hours**
Elevation Gain:	**1500 feet**
Difficulty:	**Difficult/Strenuous**
Surface:	**Service road/Trail**

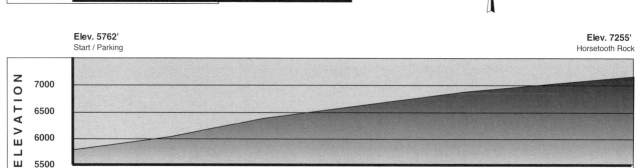

Elev. 5762'
Start / Parking

Elev. 7255'
Horsetooth Rock

ELEVATION

7000
6500
6000
5500

2.75 miles one-way   Elevation Gain: 1500'

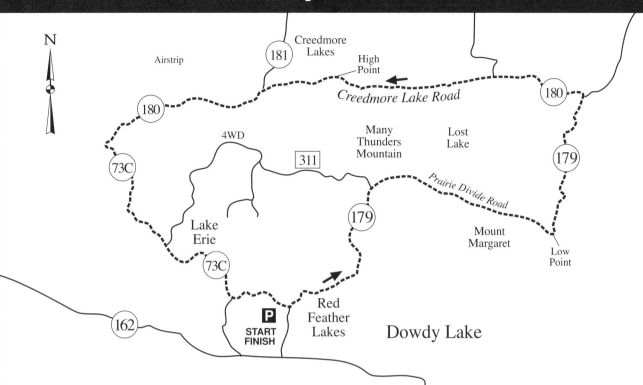

Distance:	**23.5 mile loop**
Time:	**3 to 4 hours**
Elevation Gain:	**1500 feet**
Difficulty:	**Difficult**
Surface:	**Gravel road**

■ **Directions:** From Fort Collins drive north on US 287 to CR 74E in Livermore. Turn left on CR 74E and go 24 miles to CR 179. Turn right on CR 179 and drive 0.7 miles to Red Feather Lakes.

■ **Ride:** From Red Feather Lakes, ride northeast on a paved road that, after about mile, turns to gravel. Here you begin a steep 2 mile descent to Columbine Canyon and a gradual descent along North Lone Pine Creek down to where CR 179 turns north. (This is the lowest point on the ride; the next ten miles you climb to the high point near the Creedmore Lake Road on CR 180.) Continue north 2 miles and turn left on CR 180. Fo 9 miles to 73C, an easy 6 miles ride back to Red Feather Lakes.

■ **Note:** Water is available in Red Feather Lakes.

Maps: Arapaho/Roosevelt Forest Map.
Information: Arapaho/Roosevelt Forest, Canyon Lakes Ranger District, (970) 295-6700.

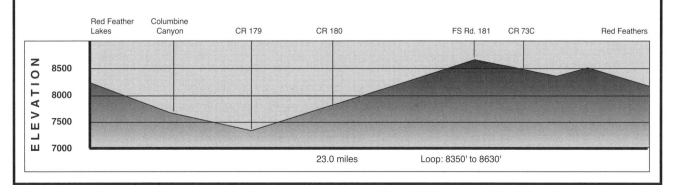

Saguache Area

Trail	Page
41. Archuleta Creek Trail	**60**
42. Bonita Hill	**61**
43. California Gulch	**62**
44. Kerber Creek	**63**
45. Luder's Creek	**64**
46. Mosquito Lake	**65**
47. Mountain Lion Creek	**66**
48. Round Mountain	**67**
49. Ute Pass	**68**

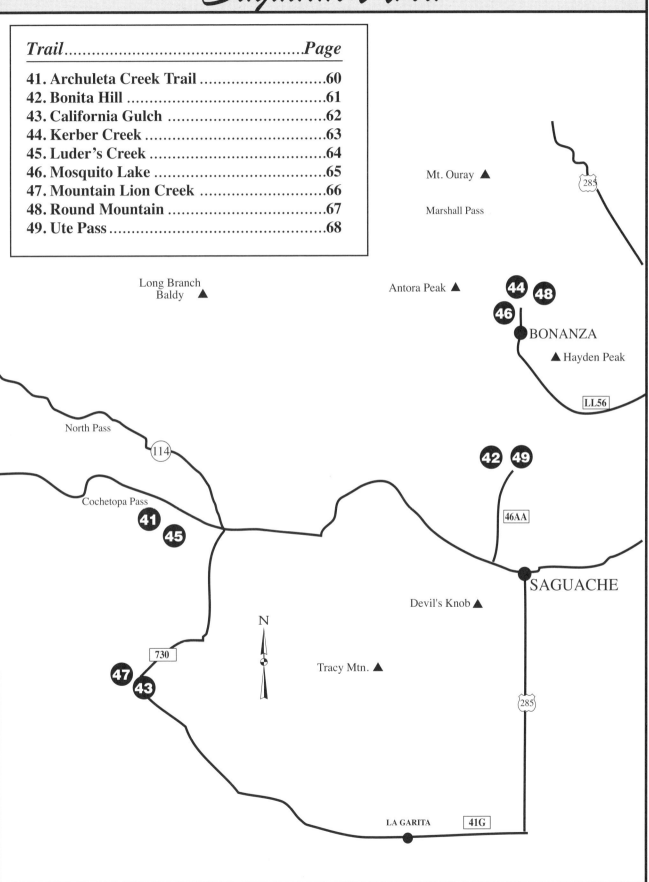

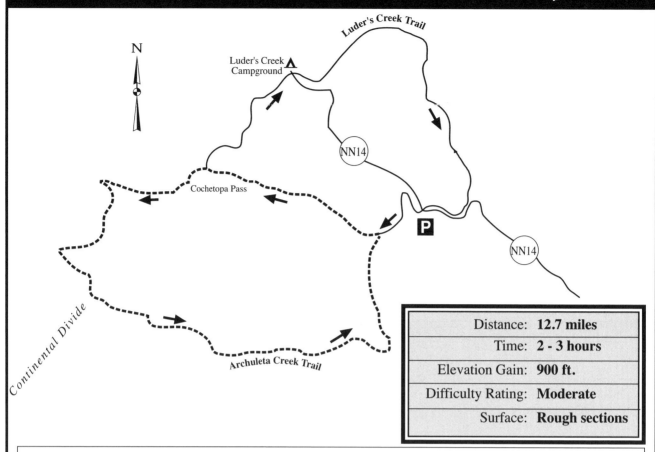

Distance:	**12.7 miles**
Time:	**2 - 3 hours**
Elevation Gain:	**900 ft.**
Difficulty Rating:	**Moderate**
Surface:	**Rough sections**

■ Directions: Follow State Hwy. 114 west from Saguache 20 miles to County Road NN14. Turn left down this road and follow six miles to Windy Point. There is a designated parking area that will access Luder's Creek Trail and Archuleta Creek Trail.

■ Description: Begin at Windy Point parking area, and proceed north down the switchback. Immediately before the first fence, turn right, and follow the logging road to Cochetopa Pass. For this trail, turn left and ride west on NN14 until you reach Archuleta Creek. Turn left across the creek and follow this road uphill through a gate. Take your first left and follow this road through two gates, then downhill to Jake's Creek Road. Turn left and ride uphill past a fence. Proceed up the switchback to the parking area.

■ Points of Interest: Once you reach Cochetopa Pass (3.2 miles), the historical markers along the Continental Divide give a sense of history to the trail. Follow NN14 downhill, but watch your speed as the turns come quickly. Once across Archuleta Creek, the trail is a bit overgrown, and can sometimes be difficult to see. If you follow the signs, maps, and directions carefully, you should not have a problem. About 8 miles into the trail, you will ride through meadows filled with beautiful wildflowers. Along these meadows are several unmarked trails. Stay on the main trail (there will be signs) because these old routes are not mapped. This trail has challenging terrain with rough surfaces. At certain times of the year gates are closed across the trail, please close gates behind you.

Maps: USGS 7.5' North Pass Quad.
Information: Rio Grande National Forest, Saguache Ranger District, (719) 655-2547.

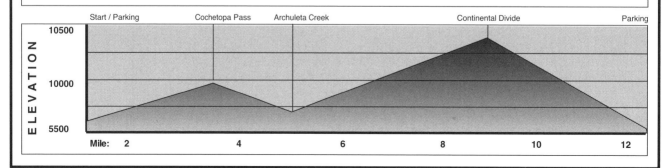

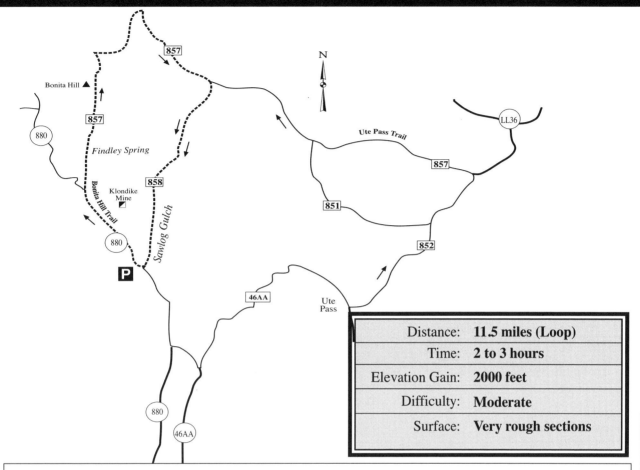

Distance:	**11.5 miles (Loop)**
Time:	**2 to 3 hours**
Elevation Gain:	**2000 feet**
Difficulty:	**Moderate**
Surface:	**Very rough sections**

■ Directions: Take State Hwy. 114 west from Saguache 1.5 miles and turn right onto Forest Service Road 880 (Findley Gulch). Follow FR 800 to the intersection with 858 (Sawlog Gulch), and park at designated area. This location will access both the Ute Pass Trail and the Bonita Hill Trail.

■ Description: Begin at parking area, and take 880 north along Findley Gulch to Bonita Hill. Turn right onto 857 and proceed to the top of Bonita Hill. Follow 857 down and then up an old jeep trail (10,400 ft). Continue on 857, and descend into Columbia Gulch. Turn right where 857 intersects 858, and cross Little Kerber Creek. Climb to the top of Sawlog Gulch, and then go 3 miles downhill to the parking area.

■ Points of Interest: The southern view from atop Bonita Hill is impressive even to natives of the San Luis Valley. The hilltop is covered with a gorgeous Aspen stands and is a great place to bring a picnic lunch. The descent after Bonita Hill is short-lived, as it is interrupted by a very steep 2-mile climb. This hill is pock-marked by abandoned mines, which are safe to look at, but from a distance! Be careful around old shafts. The downhill into Columbia Gulch is exciting, and the final descent down Sawlog Gulch is even more so, but more dangerous as well. Enjoy the meadows filled with assorted wildflowers atop Sawlog Gulch before beginning the descent since you won't have time to look on your way down! This trail consists of driveable roads and mostly smooth surfaces. There are long and sustained grades with a few stream beds that are easily crossed.

Maps: USGS 7.5' Klondike Mine and Graveyard Gulch Quads.
Information: Rio Grande National Forest, Saguache Ranger District, (719) 655-2547.

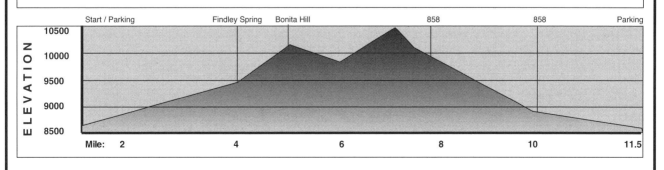

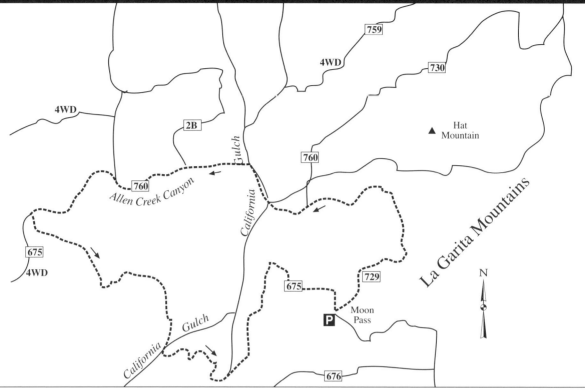

■ **Directions:** Take US Hwy. 285 south from Saguache, and turn right onto County Road 41G towards La Garita. Remain on 41G past La Garita, and turn left onto Forest Road 675 (approximately 10 miles). Follow this Road to Moon Pass and there will be a parking area with access to Mountain Lion Creek Trail and California Gulch Trail.

■ **Description:** Start from the parking area and ride down 729 to the Allen's Creek sign. Go through the gate and bear left following Allen's Creek Road to the Moon Pass sign. Turn left and follow 675 back up to the Moon Pass parking area. Road 729 is well maintained and smooth, California Gulch becomes very rough along Allen's Creek.

■ **Points of Interest:** The trail begins atop Moon Pass, and goes downhill from there. When you reach the bottom, about 4 miles later, you enter Allen's Creek Canyon, which has some good views, along with a

Distance:	**18.0 miles (Loop)**
Time:	**2 to 3 hours**
Elevation Gain:	**1600 feet**
Difficulty:	**Moderate**
Surface:	**Smooth, rough sections**

rough climb back uphill. Once you reach 675 again, the views off to the left of an extended old growth spruce-fir stand are beautiful. The final downhill back to Moon Pass parking area is fun, but the terrain is not very challenging.

Maps: USGS 7.5' Bowers Peak, Grouse Park and Lake Mountain Quads.
Information: Rio Grande National Forest, Saguache Ranger District, (719) 655-2547.

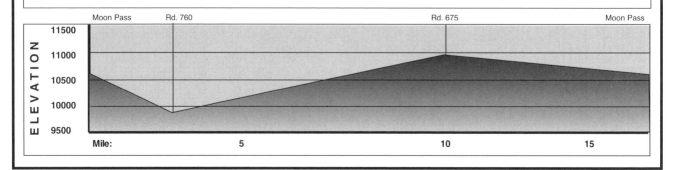

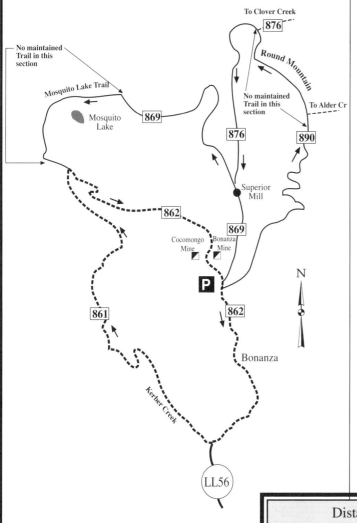

■ **Directions:** Take US Hwy. 285 from Saguache 19 miles north to Villa Grove. Turn left onto County Road LL56, follow this road another 14 miles to Bonanza, then continue about 2 miles to the intersection of Forest Roads 890 and 862. There will be a designated parking area with access to Kerber Creek Trail, Mosquito Lake Trail and Round Mountain Trail.

■ **Description:** Begin at the parking area, and go back down LL56 through Bonanza. Turn right onto 861, and follow that road about 6 miles to 862. Turn right and follow 862 around several switchbacks, past the mines, to the parking area.

■ **Points of interest:** Once you reach 861, the views are spectacular for the remainder of the ride. On 862, the downhill switchbacks a few times, so be careful not to follow the wrong route. About two thirds of the way down 862, you will come across the old Cocomongo and Bonanza mines. Stay on the trail and do not walk around near the sites, as the hills are pock marked with abandoned mine shafts. Appreciating the history of the area can be done by observing the old buildings from the road. This trail follows drive-able roads its entire length.

Maps: USGS 7.5' Bonanza Quad.
Information: Rio Grande National Forest, Saguache Ranger District, (719) 655-2547.

Distance:	**10.5 Miles**
Time:	**1.5 to 2 Hours**
Elevation Gain:	**1000 Ft.**
Difficulty Rating:	**Easy**
Surface:	**Rough sections**

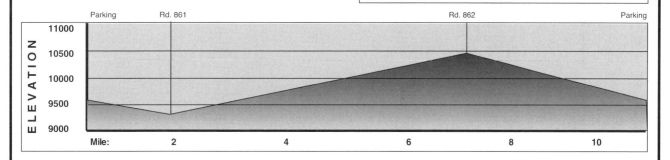

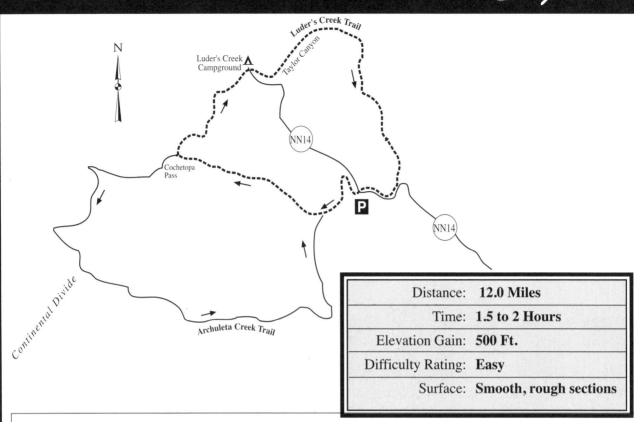

Distance:	**12.0 Miles**
Time:	**1.5 to 2 Hours**
Elevation Gain:	**500 Ft.**
Difficulty Rating:	**Easy**
Surface:	**Smooth, rough sections**

■ **Directions:** Follow State Hwy. 114 west from Saguache 20 miles to County Road NN14. Turn left down this road and follow six miles to Windy Point. There is a designated parking area with access to Luder's Creek Trail and Archuleta Creek Trail.

■ **Description:** Begin at Windy Point parking area, and head North on the switchback going downhill. Follow that road as it curves back, and turn right just before the first fence. Follow this logging road uphill until you reach NN14 again at Cochetopa Pass. Turn right and ride on this road past Luder's Creek campground. Turn left at Taylor Canyon Road and proceed along the jeep trail. The road from there becomes confusing; follow the signs carefully. Remain on Taylor Canyon Road, and follow it back to NN14. Turn right and follow the highway back to the parking area.

■ **Points of Interest:** You will reach Cochetopa Pass 3.2 miles from the parking area. Turn left over the cat-tle guard and ride 50 feet, and you will see the historical marker bearing the old stage route and elevation. At that marker, you are standing on the Continental Divide. Then turn back and follow NN14 the other way to Luder's Creek campground, a wonderful area to camp for the night if your trip allows for it. Be careful once you are on Taylor Canyon Road because there are two barbed wire fences across the trail. In order to pass, you must open the gates, and close them once you have gone through. Depending on the time of year, you may ride through a cow pasture while on this road. Proceed slowly, as some cattle may graze in the middle of the trail. And be careful not to spook the cows. This trail has few obstacles and rather shallow climbs with some rough surfaces.

Maps: USGS 7.5' North Pass Quad.
Information: Rio Grande National Forest, Saguache Ranger District, (719) 655-2547.

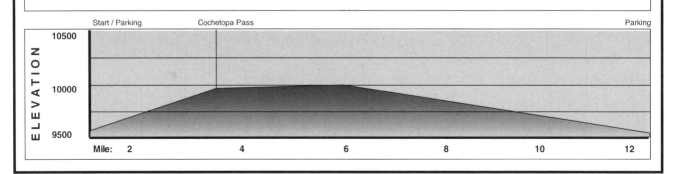

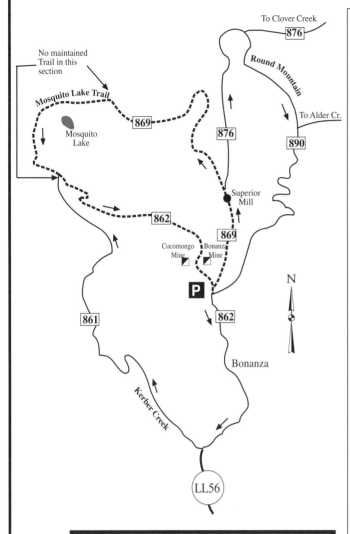

To Clover Creek
876

No maintained Trail in this section

Round Mountain

Mosquito Lake Trail

869

To Alder Cr.

876

890

Mosquito Lake

Superior Mill

862

869

Cocomongo Mine

Bonanza Mine

P

862

N

861

Bonanza

Kerber Creek

LL56

■ **Directions:** Take US Hwy. 285 from Saguache 19 miles north to Villa Grove. Turn left onto County Road LL56 and follow this road another 14 miles to Bonanza. Continue about 2 miles to the junction of Forest Roads 890 and 862. There is a designated parking with access to Kerber Creek Trail, Mosquito Lake Trail, and Round Mountain Trail.

■ **Description:** From the parking area, turn right and ride up Road 869 until you reach Superior Mill (2 miles). Bear left and follow the road uphill until you reach the Rio Grande National Forest boundary with Pike/San Isabel National Forest. Turn left down a trail and follow until you cross a creek. Turn left and follow the creek downhill to Mosquito Lake. Here the trail turns into a logging road, which you can follow to 862. Take 862 downhill to the parking area.

■ **Points of Interest:** The trail is rocky until you reach Superior Mill, which is on your right (2 miles). Near the mine, you will ride on mine tailings for about half a mile. About a mile farther, the trail cuts through an old timber cut area and then follows the divide between two the National forests down to Mosquito Lake. The trail to the lake is very rough, and difficult to discern at times. The single-track section past the creek is hard to follow, but the view of the lake is worthwhile. The climb from the lake back up to 862 is a steep logging road, but the descent back to the parking area with its forest setting and switchback trail is fun. Sections of the trail are difficult to find, so follow directions, maps, and signs carefully. Some sections are single track hiking trails, so the trail is not flat or wide and the surface tends to be rougher. Stream crossings are not difficult, but other obstacles to watch for are fallen trees and large rocks.

Maps: USGS 7.5' Bonanza Quad.
Information: Rio Grande National Forest, Saguache Ranger District, (719) 655-2547.

Distance:	**11.0 Miles (Loop)**
Time:	**2 to 3 Hours**
Elevation Gain:	**1800 ft.**
Difficulty Rating:	**Difficult**
Surface:	**Primarily rough**

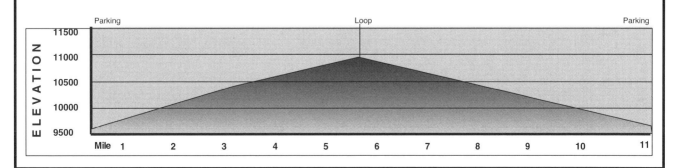

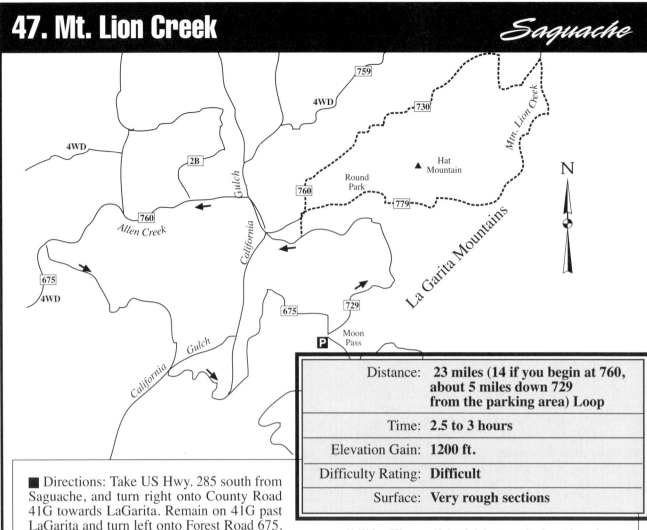

Distance:	**23 miles (14 if you begin at 760, about 5 miles down 729 from the parking area) Loop**
Time:	**2.5 to 3 hours**
Elevation Gain:	**1200 ft.**
Difficulty Rating:	**Difficult**
Surface:	**Very rough sections**

■ Directions: Take US Hwy. 285 south from Saguache, and turn right onto County Road 41G towards LaGarita. Remain on 41G past LaGarita and turn left onto Forest Road 675. Follow this road to Moon Pass, and there will be a parking area with access to Mountain Lion Creek Trail and California Gulch Trail.

■ Description: Begin at the parking area and ride down 729 to its intersection with 760. Turn right and then bear right again onto 779 and ride through Round Park to the sign for Mountain Lion Creek. Turn left at the intersection onto 730. Follow this to 760 and then back to 729. This will take you back to the parking area.

■ Points of Interest: This trail heads through Round Park, which has beautiful meadows and wildlife. The trail is fairly tough, but the views along almost every section of it are very scenic. There are a few gates across the trail, but simply opening them and remembering to close them behind you allows passage. There are a few easy creek crossings as well. The view along the trail is beautiful if you pay attention while riding.

Maps: USGS 7.5' Bowers Peak, Grouse Park and Lake Mountain Quads.
Information: Rio Grande National Forest, Saguache Ranger District, (719) 655-2547.

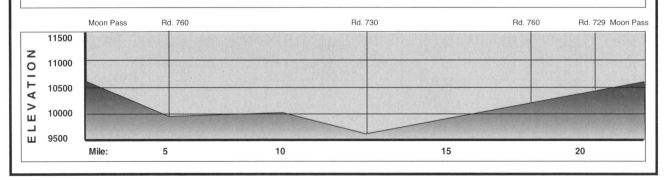

48. Round Mountain

Directions: Take US Hwy. 285 from Saguache 19 miles north to Villa Grove. Turn left onto County Road LL56. Follow this road for 14 miles to Bonanza, then continue about 2 miles to the intersection of Forest Roads 890 and 862. There will be a designated parking area with access to Kerber Creek Trail and Mosquito Lake Trail.

Description: Begin at parking area, and take Forest Road 890 up to Round Mountain. Bear left and follow the abandonded jeep trail to a clearing. Then turn left at a sharp angle onto 876. Take the road down to the intersection with 869 at Superior Mill. Head south on 869 back to the parking area.

The track has a very rough surface and an average grade of 10 percent. This climb is difficult, so be prepared. Once at the turnoff for Round Mountain, there are gorgeous alpine meadows and a terrific view down into the Rawley Gulch and Squirrel Creek regions. You will ride very close by several old mines, so be careful and stay on the trail. The downhill on 876 can be tricky. It descends quickly, and has several switchbacks that come up unexpectedly. Sections of the trail are difficult to find, so follow directions, maps, and signs carefully. Some sections are single track hiking trails so the trail is not very flat or wide and the surface tends to be rougher. Stream crossings are not difficult, but other obstacles to watch for are fallen trees and large rocks.

Maps: USGS 7 1/2' Bonanza and Whale Hill Quads.
Information: Rio Grande National Forest, Saguache Ranger District, (719) 655-2547.

Distance:	**10.8 miles**
Time:	**2 to 3 hours**
Elevation Gain:	**1800 ft.**
Difficulty Rating:	**Difficult**
Surface:	**Dirt/Primarily rough**

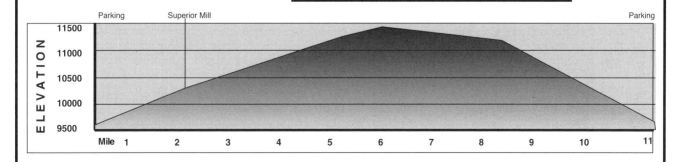

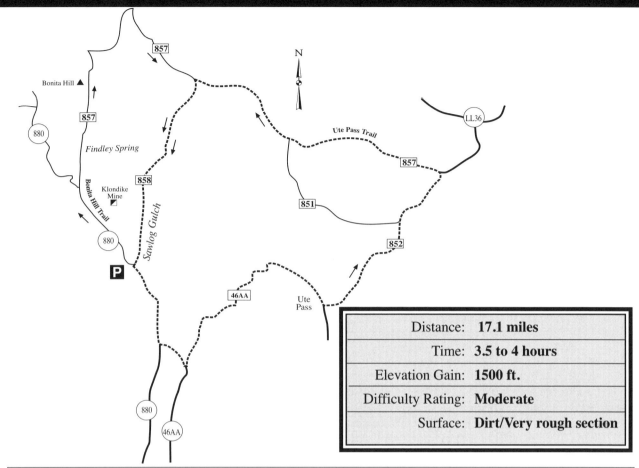

Distance:	**17.1 miles**
Time:	**3.5 to 4 hours**
Elevation Gain:	**1500 ft.**
Difficulty Rating:	**Moderate**
Surface:	**Dirt/Very rough section**

■ Directions: Take State Hwy. 114 west from Saguache 1.5 miles and turn right onto FR 880 (Findley Gulch). Follow the road to the intersection of 858 (Sawlog Gulch) and park in the designated area. The parking area has access to both the Ute Pass Trail and the Bonita Hill Trail.

■ Description: Begin at the parking area, and head south on 880. Turn left on the road with an old cabin and follow to 46AA. Turn left on 46AA, and take this road to the top of Ute Pass (5.8 miles from parking area, 9944 ft). Bear left at the pass and descend on 852 to Columbia Gulch. Turn left onto 857 and follow the road to the intersection with 858. Turn left across Little Kerber Creek and proceed up Sawlog Gulch. The half-mile climb leads to an open field, which then leads back down to the parking area (3 miles).

■ Points of Interest: The valley views while climbing Ute Pass are beautiful, and the Ute Pass downhill is enjoyable (and fast!). If you chose, turn right at Ute Pass and ride another mile uphill. You will be rewarded by an even more breathtaking scene than those who proceed directly downhill will see. Once above the pass, however, you must turn around and ride back down, and follow the directions for the descent. The cliffs and wildlife along Columbia Gulch provide a pleasant backdrop for this leg of the trip, and you can hear Little Kerber Creek gurgling as you approach. Once in Sawlog Gulch, the meadows and wildflowers provide an excellent resting place. But be extremely careful on the descent, as the trail is strewn with large rocks and ruts. This trail consists of driveable roads and mostly smooth surfaces. There are long and sustained grades with a few stream beds that are easily crossed.

Maps: USGS 7.5' Klondike Mine and Graveyard Gulch Quads.
Information: Rio Grande National Forest, Saguache Ranger District, (719) 655-2547.

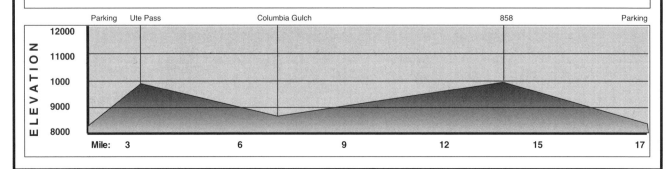

Steamboat Springs Area

Trail	*Page*
50. Buffalo Park Road	**70**
51. Fish Creek Falls	**71**
52. Lynx Pass	**72**
53. Rabbit Ears Peak	**73**
54. Steamboat to Steamboat Lake State Park	**74**

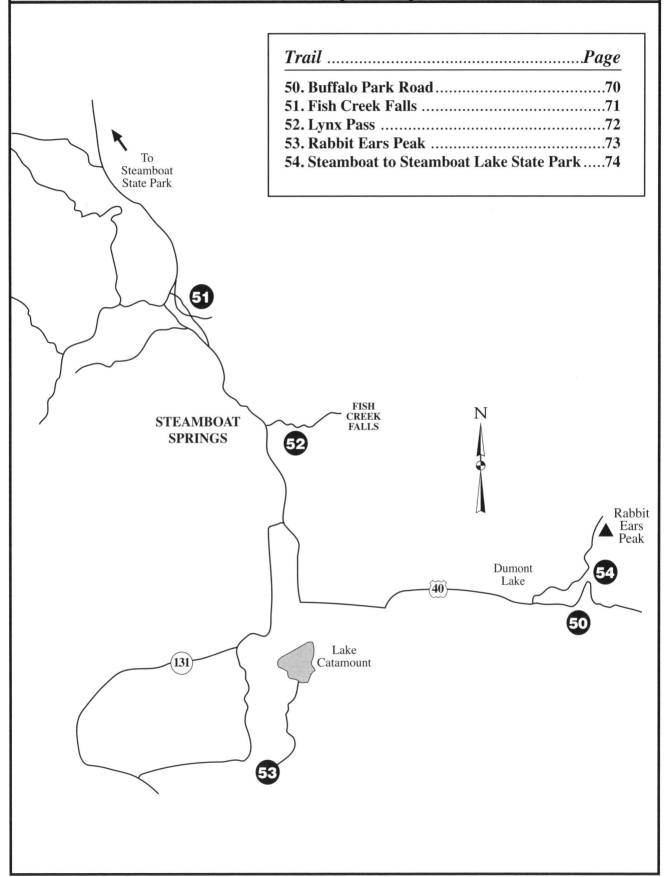

To
Steamboat
State Park

51

FISH
CREEK
FALLS

**STEAMBOAT
SPRINGS**

52

N

Rabbit
Ears
Peak

54

Dumont
Lake

(40)

50

(131)

Lake
Catamount

53

Dumont Lake
Campground

START
FINISH

14

Walton Creek
Campground

TH

Baker
Mtn.

Muddy Pass

Meadows
Campground

251

Lake
Agnes

40

Walton
Peak

Arapaho/Roosevelt

National

Forest

100

N

Basin
Reservoir

Albert
Reservoir

Buffalo
Park

Gore
Mtn.

■ Directions: Take US 40 from Steamboat Springs 21 miles to Forest Service Road 100 (1 mile past the Dumont Lake turnoff), right 100 yards to the parking area.

■ Ride: From the parking area near US 40, ride south on FR 100. The road is a lightly used, well maintained gravel road that continues past Buffalo Park to Colorado 134, a 25 mile one-way ride. The distance to Buffalo Park is 11.5 miles. There are no connecting trails from the road.

■ Note: Restrooms and water available at Dumont Lake Campground.

Maps: USGS 7.5' Rabbit Ears Peak Quad, Routt National Forest Map.
Information: Routt National Forest, Hahns Peak/Bears Ears Ranger District, (970) 879-1870.

Distance:	**23.0 miles round-trip**
Time:	**3 to 4 hours**
Elevation Gain:	**220 feet**
Difficulty:	**Easy to moderate**
Surface:	**Gravel road**

U.S. 40

Buffalo Park

ELEVATION

9400
9300
9200
9100

High Point: 9419'   11.5 miles one-way   Low Point: 9200'   Elevation Gain: 220'

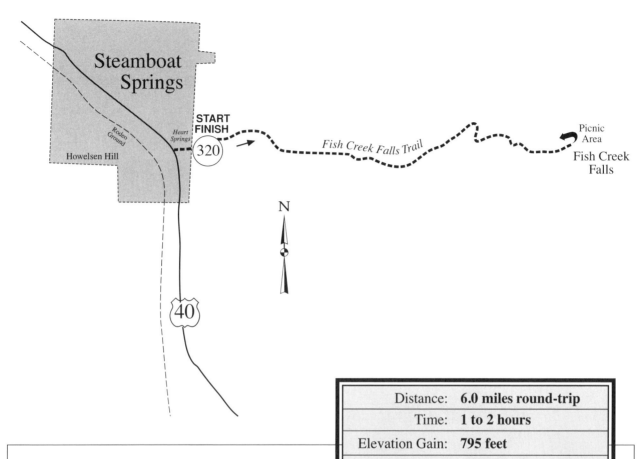

Distance:	**6.0 miles round-trip**
Time:	**1 to 2 hours**
Elevation Gain:	**795 feet**
Difficulty:	**Moderate**
Surface:	**Gravel road**

■ Ride: On Hwy 40 from Steamboat Springs, turn north onto 3rd Street, then right onto Fish Creek Falls Road. Follow the road 3 miles to the Fish Creek Falls picnic grounds. The gravel road is steep in spots, but in good condition. The waterfall makes the trip worth the ride.

■ Note: No drinking water available at the picnic grounds.

Maps: USGS 7.5' Steamboat Springs Quad.
Information: Routt National Forest, Hahns Peak/Bears Ears Ranger District, (970) 879-1870.

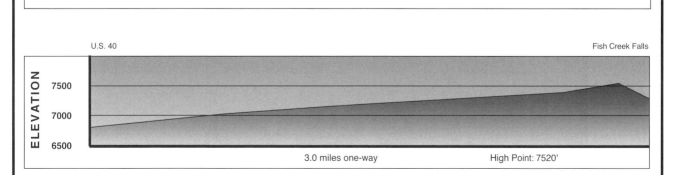

Steamboat
Springs

Fish
Creek
Falls

131

40

14

Lake
Catamount

Parking Fee
@ Stagecoach
State Park

Yellow Jacket
Pass

Stagecoach
Reservoir

CR 14

TH
START
FINISH

Morrison Creek

Stagecoach
Res. Inlet

16

N

16

Lynx
Pass

Lynx Pass
Campground

131

134

■ Directions: From Steamboat Springs, go south on U.S. 40 approximately 3.5 miles to Colorado 131. Turn right and follow 131 south 5.75 miles to County Road 14. Turn left onto County Road 14, travel over Yellow Jacket Pass to County Road 16, about 6 miles south of road 131 and just past Stagecoach Reservoir.

■ Ride: From County Road 14, turn left at the bridge to County Road 16 (the road follows Little Morrison Creek up to near Lynx Pass). Follow the trail southeast for 16 miles, a gradual climb on a well-maintained road to Lynx Pass Campground.

■ Note: There are toilets, well water, and a small lake at the campground.

Maps: Routt National Forest Map.
Information: Routt National Forest, Yampa Ranger District, (970) 638-4516

Distance:	**32.0 miles**
Time:	**4 to 6 hours**
Elevation Gain:	**1750 feet**
Difficulty:	**Moderate**
Surface:	**Gravel road**

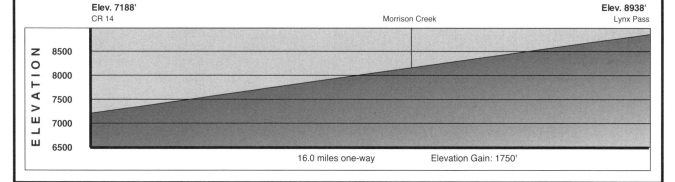

Elev. 7188'
CR 14

Morrison Creek

Elev. 8938'
Lynx Pass

ELEVATION

8500
8000
7500
7000
6500

16.0 miles one-way   Elevation Gain: 1750'

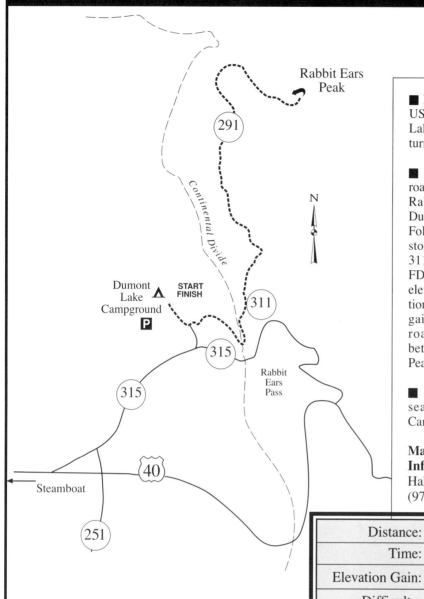

■ **Directions:** From Steamboat Springs on US 40 go south 21 miles to the Dumont Lake turnoff (Forest Service Road 315), turn left and park in the designated lot.

■ **Ride:** Take FR 291, a 4WD service road, from Dumont Lake Campground to Rabbit Ears Peak. Follow the road past Dumont Lake to the paved road FDR 315. Follow the paved road and turn left at the stone monument, FDR 311. Follow FDR 311 a short distance and turn right onto FDR 291 up to the peak. Dumont Lake elevation is 9,573 feet, Rabbit Ears elevation is 10,654 feet, a 1,080 feet elevation gain in only two miles. This is a steep road that becomes extremely steep between Dumont Lake and Rabbit Ears Peak.

■ **Note:** Drinking water and restrooms seasonally available at Dumont Lake Campground.

Maps: Routt National Forest Map.
Information: Routt National Forest, Hahns Peak/Bears Ears Ranger District, (970) 879-1870.

Distance:	**8.0 miles round-trip**
Time:	**1 to 2 hours**
Elevation Gain:	**1,080 feet**
Difficulty:	**Moderate/Strenuous**
Surface:	**Dirt Forest Service Road**

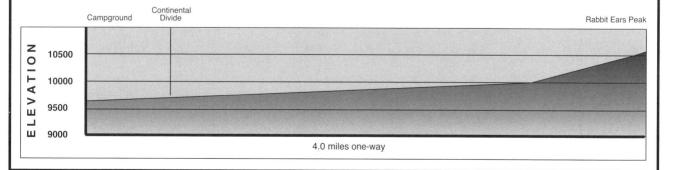

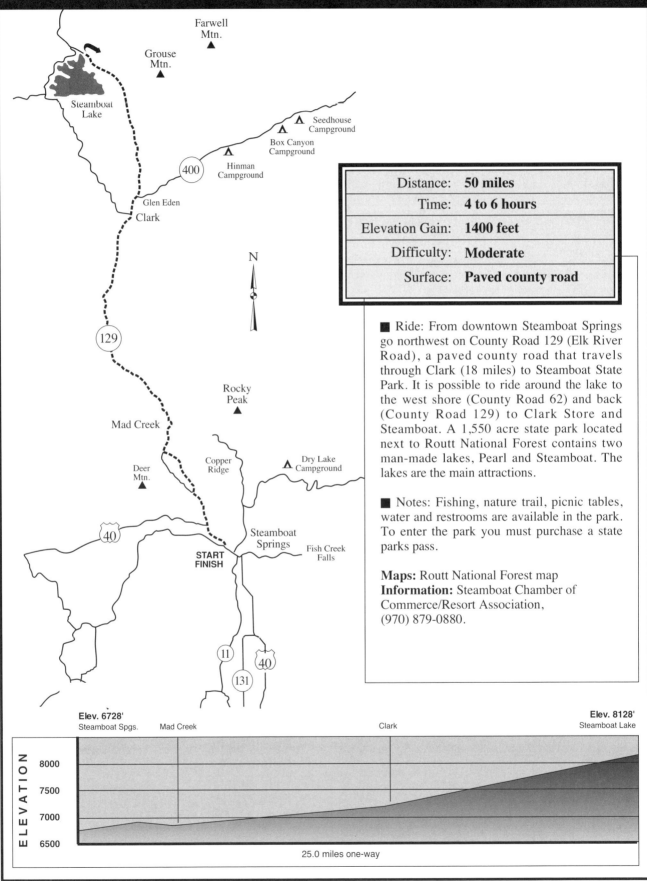

Distance:	**50 miles**
Time:	**4 to 6 hours**
Elevation Gain:	**1400 feet**
Difficulty:	**Moderate**
Surface:	**Paved county road**

■ Ride: From downtown Steamboat Springs go northwest on County Road 129 (Elk River Road), a paved county road that travels through Clark (18 miles) to Steamboat State Park. It is possible to ride around the lake to the west shore (County Road 62) and back (County Road 129) to Clark Store and Steamboat. A 1,550 acre state park located next to Routt National Forest contains two man-made lakes, Pearl and Steamboat. The lakes are the main attractions.

■ Notes: Fishing, nature trail, picnic tables, water and restrooms are available in the park. To enter the park you must purchase a state parks pass.

Maps: Routt National Forest map
Information: Steamboat Chamber of Commerce/Resort Association, (970) 879-0880.

Elev. 6728'
Steamboat Spgs.   Mad Creek

Elev. 8128'
Steamboat Lake

Clark

25.0 miles one-way

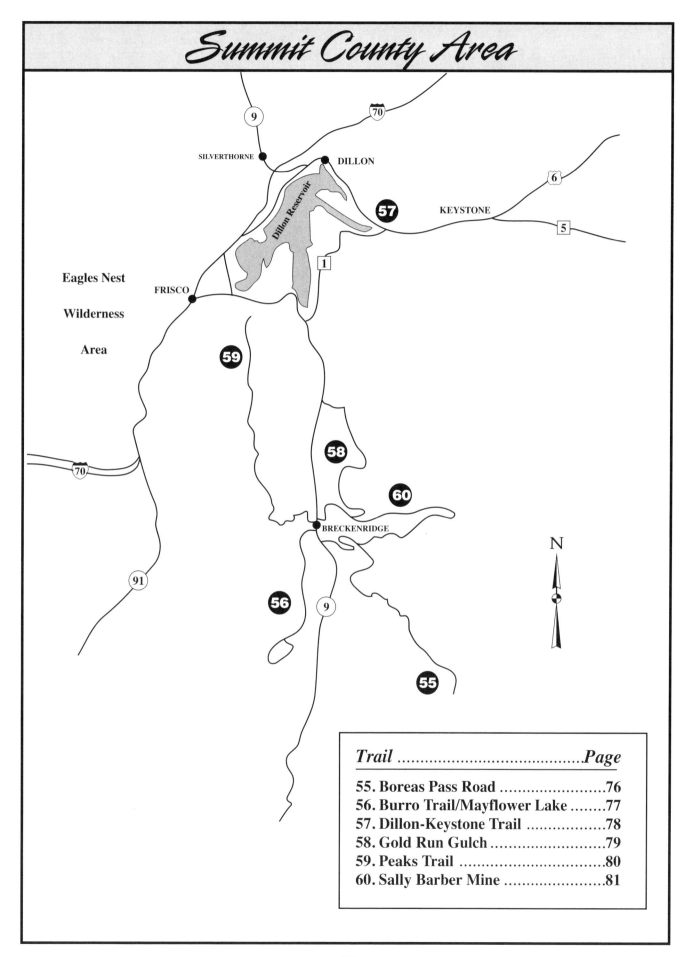

Summit County Area

SILVERTHORNE

DILLON

⑨

⑦⓪

⑥

KEYSTONE

5

57

Dillon Reservoir

1

Eagles Nest

FRISCO

Wilderness

Area

59

⑦⓪

58

60

91

BRECKENRIDGE

56

⑨

55

N

Trail	Page
55. Boreas Pass Road	76
56. Burro Trail/Mayflower Lake	77
57. Dillon-Keystone Trail	78
58. Gold Run Gulch	79
59. Peaks Trail	80
60. Sally Barber Mine	81

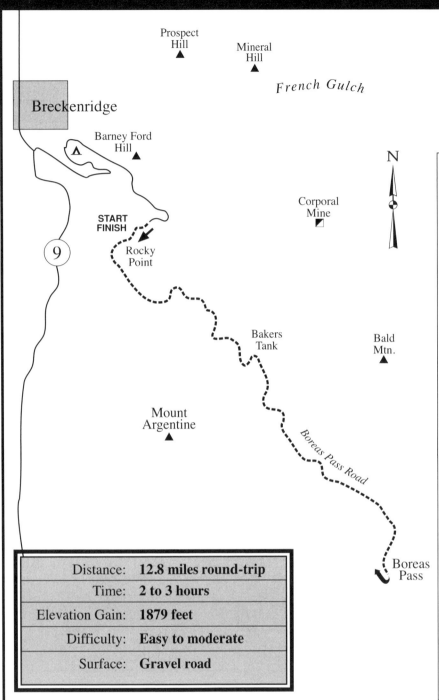

Prospect Hill ▲

Mineral Hill ▲

French Gulch

Breckenridge

Barney Ford Hill ▲

⚑

Corporal Mine ◪

N

START FINISH

Rocky Point

⑨

Bakers Tank

Bald Mtn. ▲

Mount Argentine ▲

Boreas Pass Road

Boreas Pass

■ **Directions:** From Breckenridge turn left onto the Boreas Pass Road (Summit County Road 10) and drive approximately 3.5 miles until the pavement ends at the Forest Service sign. Park off the road.

■ **Ride:** The road from the Arapaho/Roosevelt National Forest boundary to Boreas Pass on the Continental Divide is a well-maintained, smooth gravel road. A moderately steady climb on this old railroad bed is an excellent introduction to mountain biking. A half-way marker is Bakers Tank at 3 miles, while Boreas Pass is 6.4 miles. The road continues to Como.

■ **Note:** No drinking water available along this ride. Boreas Pass elevation is 11,481 feet and is above timberline, plan ahead for the ride.

Maps: USGS 7.5' Breckenridge and Boreas Pass Quads, White River National Forest Map.
Information: White River National Forest, Dillon Ranger District, (970) 468-5400.

Distance:	**12.8 miles round-trip**
Time:	**2 to 3 hours**
Elevation Gain:	**1879 feet**
Difficulty:	**Easy to moderate**
Surface:	**Gravel road**

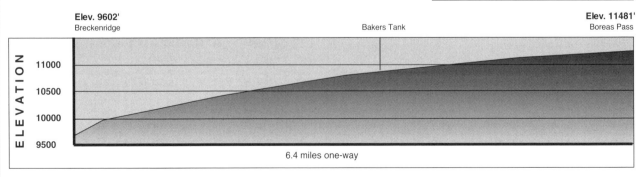

Elev. 9602'
Breckenridge

Bakers Tank

Elev. 11481'
Boreas Pass

ELEVATION
11000
10500
10000
9500

6.4 miles one-way

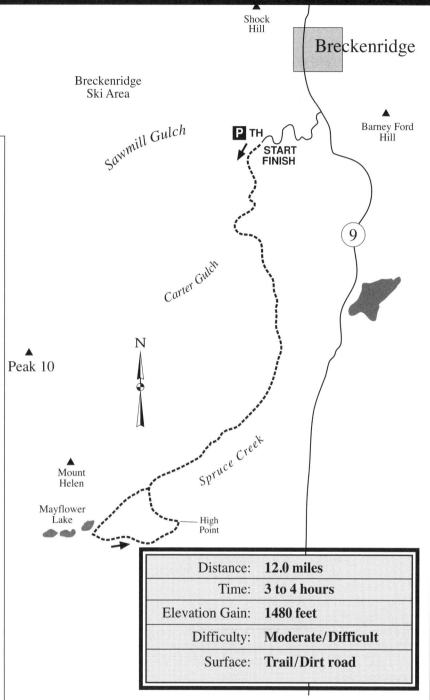

■ **Directions:** From Colorado 9 in Breckenridge, go right at the Bell Tower Mall onto South Park Street. Turn left on Village Road and continue to Beaver Run Resort. Park at the parking area, on the left, just before the resort.

■ **Ride:** Begin the Burro Trail ride at the south end of the parking lot, next to the ski slope, at the Forest Service trailhead sign. Follow a dirt road under the ski lift to the trailhead sign at the other side of the ski run. The main trail is marked by blue diamonds; follow the diamonds to Mayflower Lakes. The trail near the lakes has a steep section that can force you to walk. Other sections of the trail have stream crossings, rocky sections, and the ride is almost a continuous climb. At Mayflower Lakes, turn around and return the way you came or descend using an alternate route.

■ **Note:** Some technical riding skills recommended.

Maps: USGS 7.5' Breckenridge and Boreas Pass Quads, White River National Forest Map.
Information: White River National Forest, Dillon Ranger District, (970) 468-5400.

Distance:	**12.0 miles**
Time:	**3 to 4 hours**
Elevation Gain:	**1480 feet**
Difficulty:	**Moderate/Difficult**
Surface:	**Trail/Dirt road**

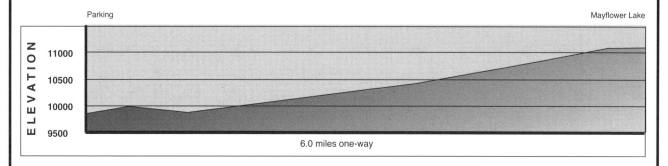

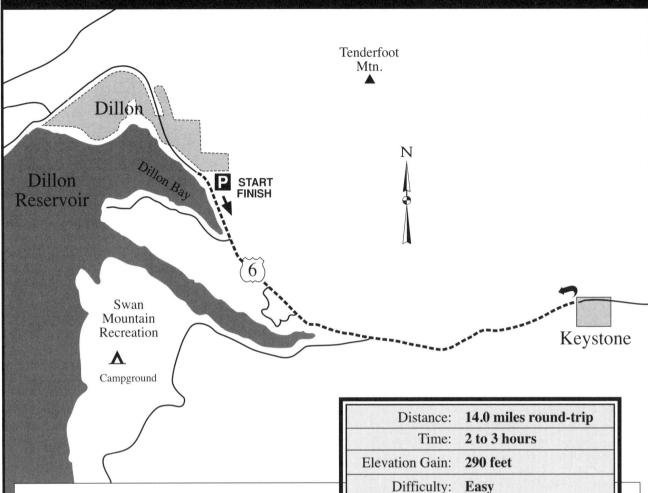

Distance:	**14.0 miles round-trip**
Time:	**2 to 3 hours**
Elevation Gain:	**290 feet**
Difficulty:	**Easy**
Surface:	**Paved path**

■ Directions: From Tenderfoot Trailhead at US 6 and Tenderfoot Street on the east side of Lake Dillon.

■ Ride: From the Tenderfoot Road Trailhead the bike path runs parallel to US 6 to Swan Mountain Road. Turn left onto Swan Mountain Road and follow the bike route signs to Soda Ridge Road. Follow Soda Ridge Road to the wooden gate where the road becomes the bike path to Keystone. Trail through meadows, forests, and wetlands along Snake River, adjacent to botanical preserve at Keystone Science School; access to National Forest trails. Return from Keystone along the same route.

Information: Summit County Chamber of Commerce, (970) 668-205.

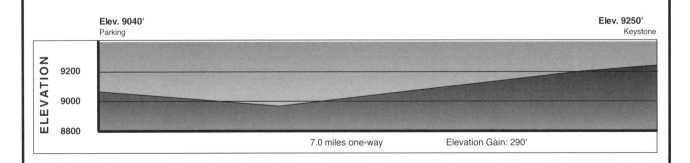

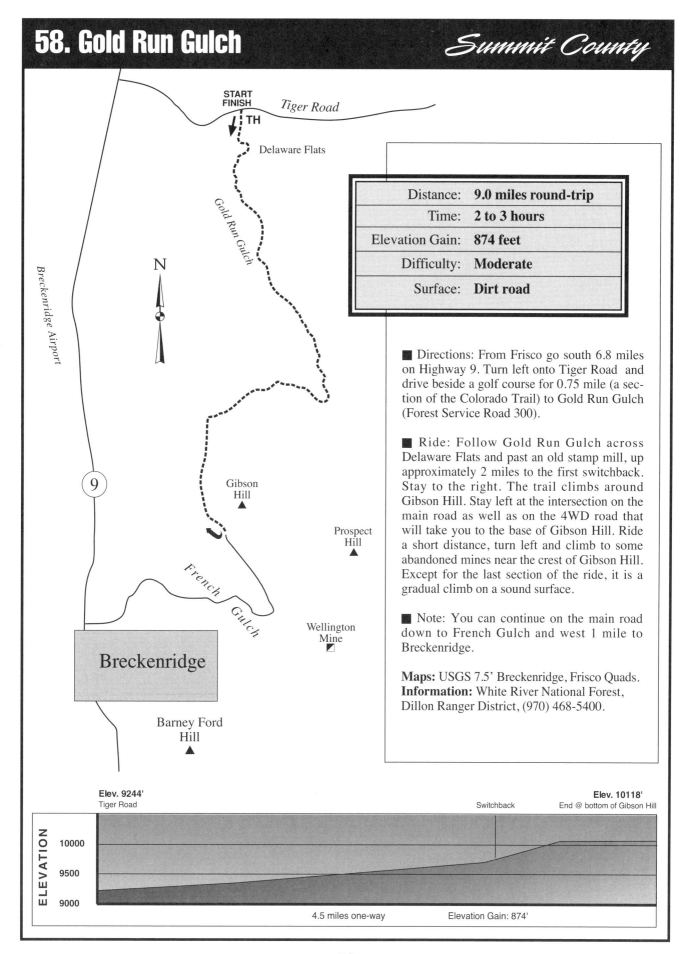

START
FINISH

Tiger Road

TH

Delaware Flats

Gold Run Gulch

N

Breckenridge Airport

9

Gibson Hill ▲

Prospect Hill ▲

French Gulch

Wellington Mine ◹

Breckenridge

Barney Ford Hill ▲

Distance:	**9.0 miles round-trip**
Time:	**2 to 3 hours**
Elevation Gain:	**874 feet**
Difficulty:	**Moderate**
Surface:	**Dirt road**

■ Directions: From Frisco go south 6.8 miles on Highway 9. Turn left onto Tiger Road and drive beside a golf course for 0.75 mile (a section of the Colorado Trail) to Gold Run Gulch (Forest Service Road 300).

■ Ride: Follow Gold Run Gulch across Delaware Flats and past an old stamp mill, up approximately 2 miles to the first switchback. Stay to the right. The trail climbs around Gibson Hill. Stay left at the intersection on the main road as well as on the 4WD road that will take you to the base of Gibson Hill. Ride a short distance, turn left and climb to some abandoned mines near the crest of Gibson Hill. Except for the last section of the ride, it is a gradual climb on a sound surface.

■ Note: You can continue on the main road down to French Gulch and west 1 mile to Breckenridge.

Maps: USGS 7.5' Breckenridge, Frisco Quads.
Information: White River National Forest, Dillon Ranger District, (970) 468-5400.

Elev. 9244'
Tiger Road

Elev. 10118'
End @ bottom of Gibson Hill

Switchback

ELEVATION

10000
9500
9000

4.5 miles one-way   Elevation Gain: 874'

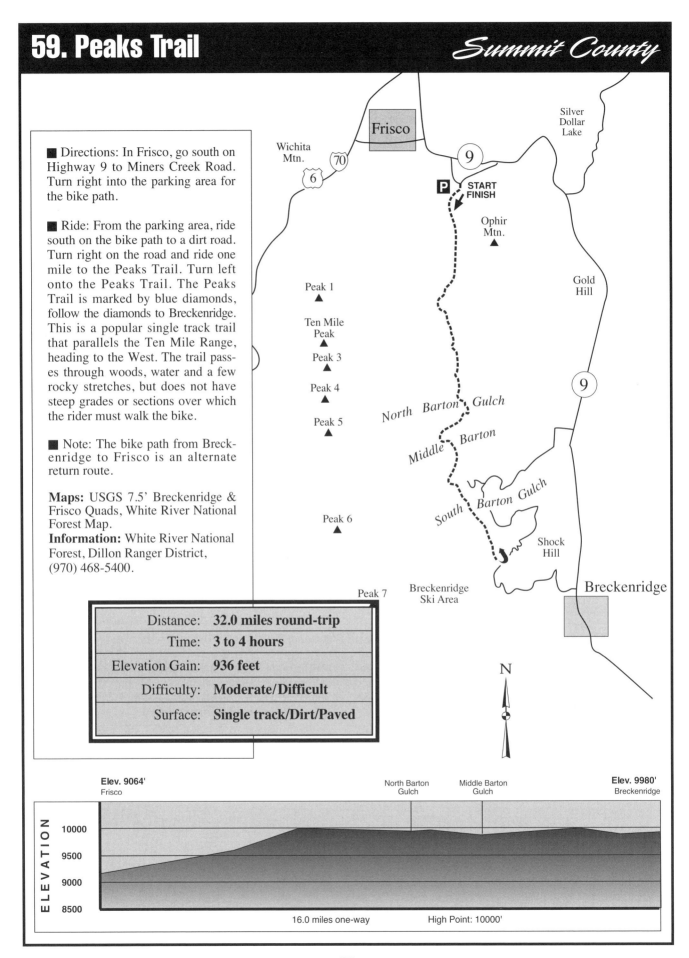

Directions: In Frisco, go south on Highway 9 to Miners Creek Road. Turn right into the parking area for the bike path.

Ride: From the parking area, ride south on the bike path to a dirt road. Turn right on the road and ride one mile to the Peaks Trail. Turn left onto the Peaks Trail. The Peaks Trail is marked by blue diamonds, follow the diamonds to Breckenridge. This is a popular single track trail that parallels the Ten Mile Range, heading to the West. The trail passes through woods, water and a few rocky stretches, but does not have steep grades or sections over which the rider must walk the bike.

Note: The bike path from Breckenridge to Frisco is an alternate return route.

Maps: USGS 7.5' Breckenridge & Frisco Quads, White River National Forest Map.
Information: White River National Forest, Dillon Ranger District, (970) 468-5400.

Distance:	**32.0 miles round-trip**
Time:	**3 to 4 hours**
Elevation Gain:	**936 feet**
Difficulty:	**Moderate/Difficult**
Surface:	**Single track/Dirt/Paved**

Silver Dollar Lake

Frisco

Wichita Mtn.

Ophir Mtn.

Gold Hill

Peak 1

Ten Mile Peak

Peak 3

Peak 4

Peak 5

North Barton Gulch

Middle Barton

South Barton Gulch

Shock Hill

Peak 6

Breckenridge Ski Area

Breckenridge

Peak 7

N

Elev. 9064'
Frisco

North Barton Gulch

Middle Barton Gulch

Elev. 9980'
Breckenridge

ELEVATION

10000
9500
9000
8500

16.0 miles one-way   High Point: 10000'

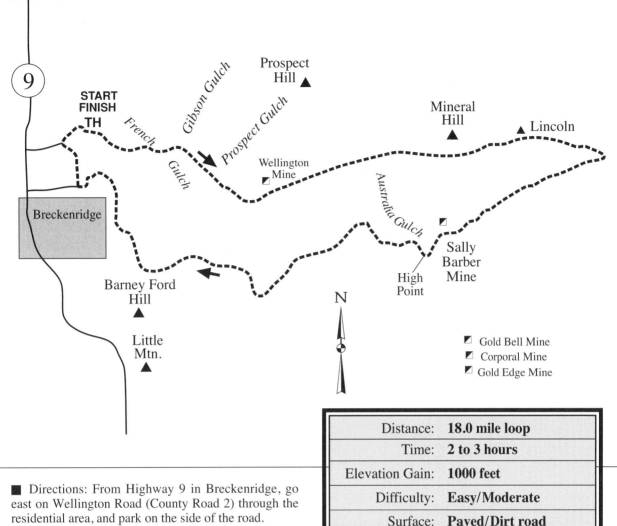

Distance:	**18.0 mile loop**
Time:	**2 to 3 hours**
Elevation Gain:	**1000 feet**
Difficulty:	**Easy/Moderate**
Surface:	**Paved/Dirt road**

■ Directions: From Highway 9 in Breckenridge, go east on Wellington Road (County Road 2) through the residential area, and park on the side of the road.

■ Ride: This easy to moderate 10-mile ride on a well-maintained, dirt road passes the Wellington Mine site and the old Lincoln town site before climbing to the Sally Barber mine site. It is a steady climb to the highest point on the ride at the Sally Barber Mine, and from that point the ride is a gradual descent back to your vehicle.

■ Note: Automobile traffic can be heavy.

Maps: White River National Forest Map.
Information: White River National Forest, Dillon Ranger District, (970) 468-5400, Summit County Chamber of Commerce, (970) 668-205.

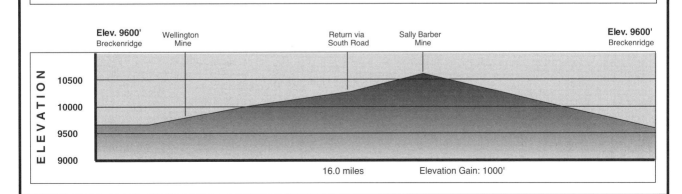

Vail Area

Trail...Page

61. Berry Creek 84
62. Camp Hale to Ptarmigan Pass 85
63. Davos 86
64. Homestake Reservoir 87
65. Lost Lake...88
66. Meadow Mountain 89
67. Mill Creek 90
68. Piney Lake...91
69. Two Elk 92
70. Vail Pass to Redcliff 93
71. Vail Pass to Ten Mile Canyon Nat. Rec. ..94
72. Village Trail and Grand Traverse 95

N

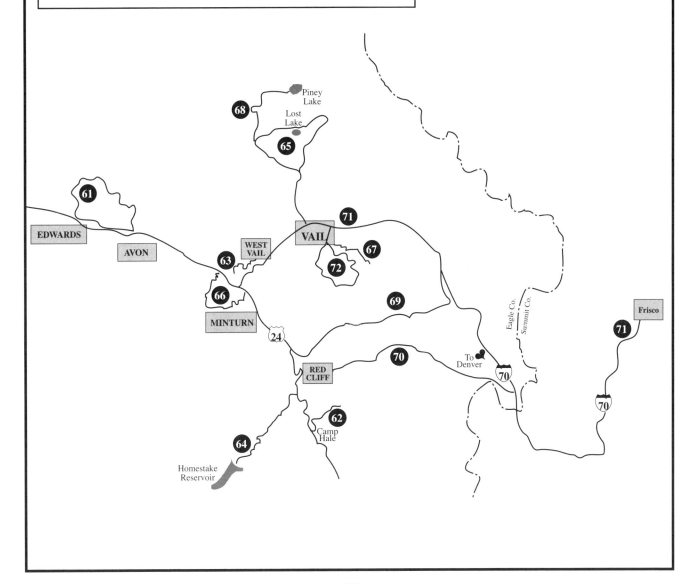

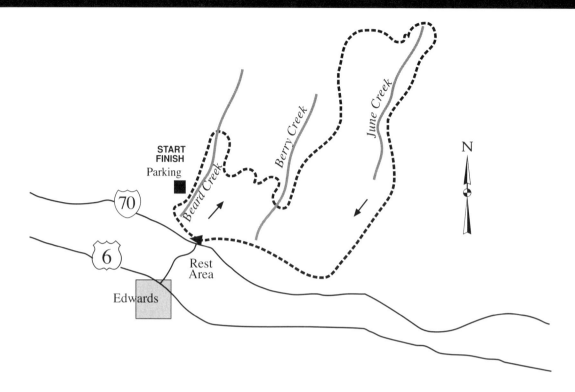

Distance:	**8.5 mile loop**
Time:	**1 to 2 hours**
Elevation Gain:	**960 feet**
Difficulty:	**Moderate**
Surface:	**Paved road/Trail**

■ Directions: From West Vail, go west on I-70 for 10 miles to Edwards (Exit 163), then travel south 0.5 mile to the Blue Memorial Rest Area in Edwards.

■ Ride: From the rest area, ride under I-70, then left on Beard Creek Road. Stay right following Berry Creek up to a switchback, and from the switchback, continue up on along a 4WD road through a series of switchbacks. Stay right past another 4WD road to the top of the ride on the main road. Follow the road down to the June Creek Road. Turn right and travel along-side June Creek past the golf course to Berry Creek Road. Turn right to return to the rest area.

■ Note: There are a number of 4WD roads at the top of the ride. Stay on main road for this ride.

Maps: USGS 7.5' Edwards Quad, White River Forest Service Map.
Information: White River National Forest, Holy Cross Ranger District, (970) 827-5715.

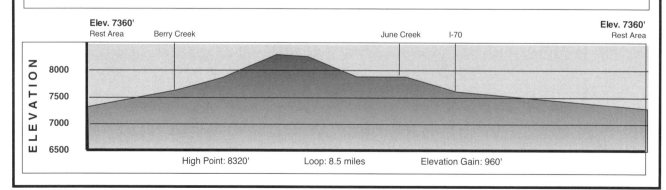

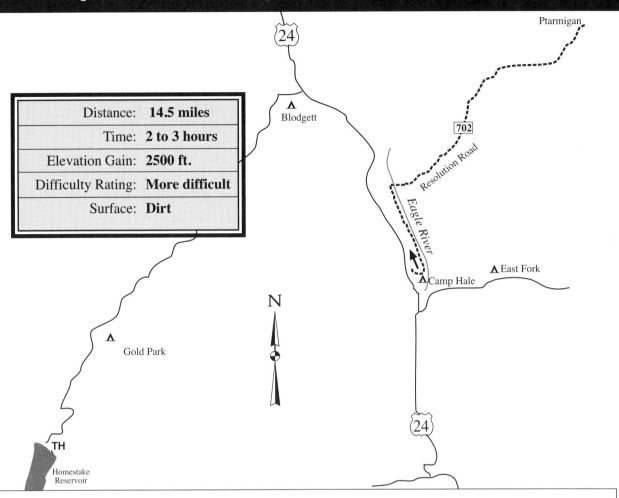

Distance:	**14.5 miles**
Time:	**2 to 3 hours**
Elevation Gain:	**2500 ft.**
Difficulty Rating:	**More difficult**
Surface:	**Dirt**

■ Directions: From Vail, travel west on 1-70 to Exit 171 for Minturn and Hwy 24. Exit here, turn left and continue south on Hwy 24 for 17 miles. Turn left at the Camp Hale Memorial sign. Park where available.

■ Ride: The ride begins at the entrance to Camp Hale. Follow the road into the camp. Take a left when the road splits. Travel one mile on this road, which parallels the Eagle River. Turn right onto Resolution Road #702, and stay to the left when the road forks at the East Fork of the Eagle River Road. Resolution Road #702 will take you to the summit at Ptarmigan Pass.

■ The first 4 miles of the ride are a steady climb. The road then steepens to a challenging climb. At this point, it is a good time to take a scenery break. The openness of this road makes it perfect for viewing the Mount of the Holy Cross as well as Notch Mountain. At the top of the road the elevation is 11,765 feet. From this location you can see the Gore Range to the east, the Sawatch Range to the west as well as the Ten-Mile Range. The ride back to your vehicle is a fast downhill. Use caution and be aware of potholes, corrucations, and other vehicles, especially other bikers.

Maps: USGS 7.5' Pando Quad.
Information: White River National Forest, Holy Cross Ranger District, (970) 827-5715.

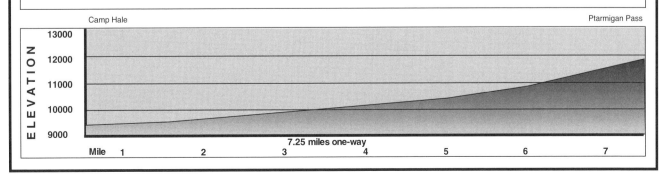

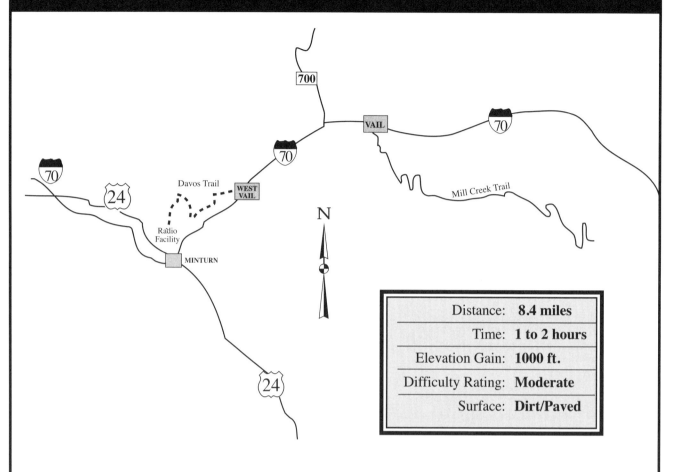

Distance:	**8.4 miles**
Time:	**1 to 2 hours**
Elevation Gain:	**1000 ft.**
Difficulty Rating:	**Moderate**
Surface:	**Dirt/Paved**

■ **Directions:** Begin the ride near the West Vail shopping center, where the bikeway ends. Ride along the frontage road heading west, then turn right on Chamonix Road. Continue along to Arosa Drive and turn right, stay to the right onto Cortina Lane until it dead ends at a dirt road.

■ **Ride:** This ride is an out and back with a few difficult but short climbs and a moderate and constant elevation gain. It is known as the Davos Hill or Radio Tower ride. The trail is a dirt 4WD road that has scattered rocks on it. The ride takes you through some large aspen glens and open meadows with a view of Dowds Junction. Continue along the rolling road and

bear left at the fork at 3.9 miles. This road takes you to the radio tower overlook, which is the turn around point of this ride. Stop here for views of Minturn, Gilman, Notch Mountain, Mount of the Holy Cross and Meadow Mountain to the south. To the west is Avon, Eagle-Vail and Edwards. To the east is the Vail ski area. Now it is a short, easy ride downhill back to West Vail.

Maps: USGS 7.5' Vail West and Minturn Quads.
Information: White River National Forest, Holy Cross Ranger District, (970) 827-5715.

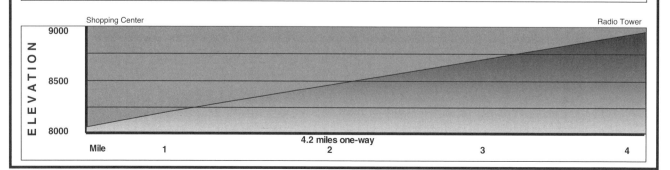

64. Homestake Reservoir

Distance:	**16.8 miles round-trip**
Time:	**1 to 2 hours**
Elevation Gain:	**1200 ft.**
Difficulty Rating:	**Moderate**
Surface:	**Dirt**

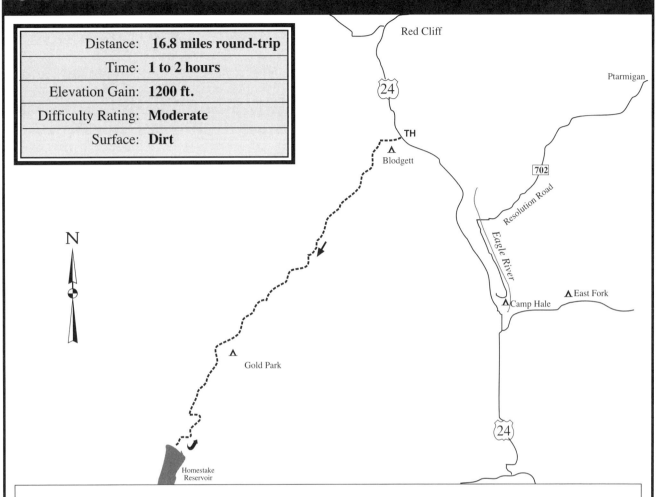

■ Directions: From Vail travel west on 1-70 to Exit 171 for Minturn, Leadville and Hwy 24. Exit here and turn left. Travel 12 miles to Homestake Road #703. Turn right and drive about one mile until you can park on the right at an old campground. Do not leave your vehicle in Blodgett Campground.

■ Ride: The ride is a series of rolling hills along a dirt road. There are several steep climbs along the way. Homestake Road parallels the Homestake Creek. The road can be quite dusty and is usually corrugated. At 6.8 miles, you will pass Gold Park Campground. Holy Cross City Road is at at the 7.2 mile point. This jeep trail is another of the area's mountain bike trails, but is probably one of the most challenging. Continue on Homestake Road for another two miles. When you reach the base of the dam, take the left most trail to the top of the dam. The reservoir is the water source for Colorado Springs.

■ The reservoir is a popular fishing spot. Take your time and walk around the dam and rest up for your trek back to your vehicle. The trip back is mostly downhill. The grade is not steep enough to coast all the way back, and there are a few climbs along the way as well.

Maps: USGS 7.5' Pando, Homestake Reservoir, and Mount of the Holy Cross Quads.
Information: White River National Forest, Holy Cross Ranger District, (970) 827-5715.

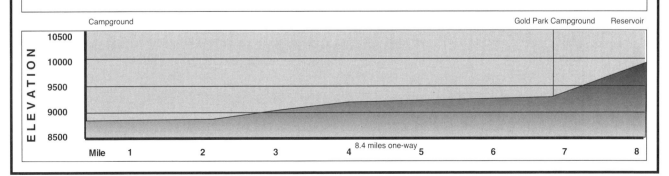

■ Directions: From Vail on the paved West Vail Bikeway, go east to Red Sandstone Road (Forest Service Road 700).

■ Ride: Take Red Sandstone Road 2.7 miles to the junction with Lost Lake Motorized Trail (FR 786), and turn right. The ride is a gradual climb on a smooth road to Lost Lake, staying left on FR 786. Approximately 4 miles from the junction, turn left onto the Lost Lake Trail (1893), follow the trail down for 3.4 miles to Red Sandstone Road (FR 700). This road takes you back to Vail, completing the loop. Lost Lake Trail is a single track trail that will test your riding skills with rocky sections and bogs.

■ Note: This trail is heavily used.

Maps: USGS 7.5' Vail West, White River National Forest Map.
Information: White River National Forest, Holy Cross Ranger District, (970) 827-5715.

Distance:	**12.0 mile loop**
Time:	**3 to 4 hours**
Elevation Gain:	**1928 feet**
Difficulty:	**Difficult**
Surface:	**Pavement/Dirt road/ Single track**

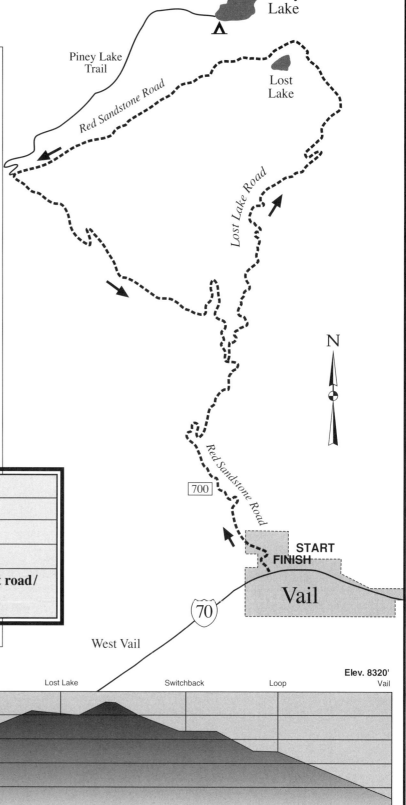

High Point: 10248' Loop: 12.0 miles Elevation Gain: 1928'

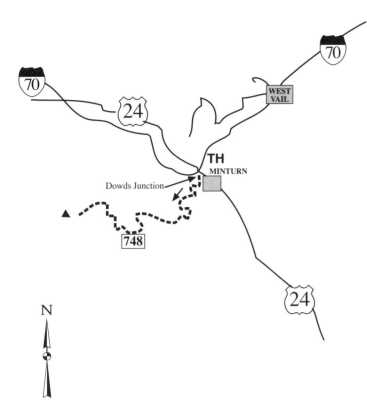

Distance:	**7 miles round trip**
Time:	**1 to 2 hours**
Elevation Gain:	**1920 ft.**
Difficulty Rating:	**Difficult**
Surface:	**Dirt**

■ Directions: Travel west on 1-70 to Exit 171 for Minturn, Leadville, and Hwy 24. Exit here and turn left. Just past the interstate there is a large dirt parking lot on the right. Park here.

■ Ride: From the trailhead sign, follow the old road that winds behind the white house at the end of the parking lot. This road climbs gradually through large open meadows and Spruce-Fir forests. The open meadows are old lettuce growing sites from back in the 1920's.

■ When you reach the fork in the road (2.7 miles up), bear right along the road marked #748. After a series of steep switchbacks, you will enter an old clear-cut site. Bear to the left here, where the road continues upwards. Ride on the double track until you reach the old sheep herders shack. There is a single track trail on the east (right) side of the shack. The trail continues to the west past a small pond. Return along the same route.

Map: USGS 7.5' Minturn Quad.
Information: White River National Forest, Holy Cross Ranger District, (970) 827-5715.

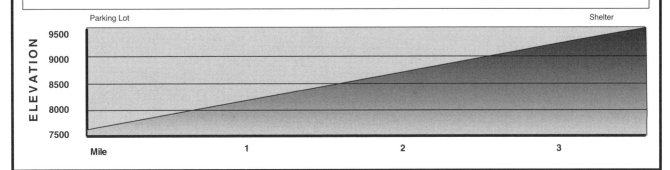

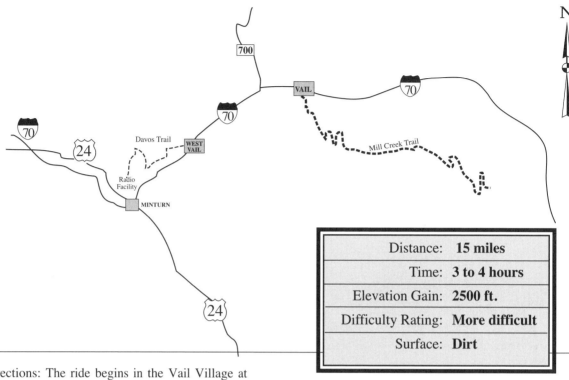

Distance:	**15 miles**
Time:	**3 to 4 hours**
Elevation Gain:	**2500 ft.**
Difficulty Rating:	**More difficult**
Surface:	**Dirt**

■ Directions: The ride begins in the Vail Village at the base of the Vista Bahn Express lift. This lift is located at the top of Bridge Street.

■ Ride: The ride begins here at the ski area's service road. Follow the road upwards as it traverses the slopes. The beginning of this trail crosses the International run, one of the steepest, fastest runs on the mountain. The first fork in the road branches off to Lionshead. Take a left here. As the road continues upwards, take another left at the next fork. The road then travels away from the village area and heads east towards Gold Peak. The road continues switchbacking across the slopes. Continue along this road, which turns away from the front of the mountain and heads in towards Mill Creek Valley. At 3.5 miles, you will reach a fork in the road; take the left-hand road. This will take you up Mill Creek. The right fork goes past Chair 10 (which you can see from this point), and then up to Mid-Vail. The road becomes a jeep trail that is passable only by high-clearance vehicles. It is passable for mountain bikers. The ride continues upwards for another 3.5 miles from the fork at Chair 10. The road parallels Mill Creek. The ride ends at a road gate.

If you are extra ambitious, you can continue on to the Commando Run, which takes you to the Shrine Pass Road and eventually to Vail Pass Rest Area. However, maps and a compass are essential for this ride. For the rest of us, take a break and enjoy the views of Gore Creek, the Mount of the Holy Cross and the Back Bowls of Vail. From here it is a simple matter of pointing your bike downhill and hanging on. Be sure to use caution and be aware of motorized traffic on the roads.

Maps: USGS 7.5' Vail East and Red Cliff Quads.
Information: White River National Forest, Holy Cross Ranger District, (970) 827-5715.

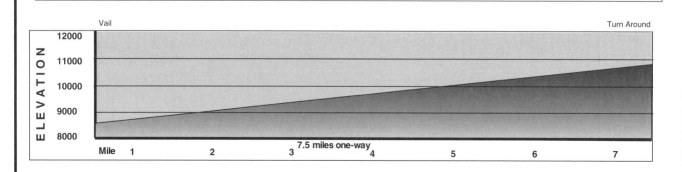

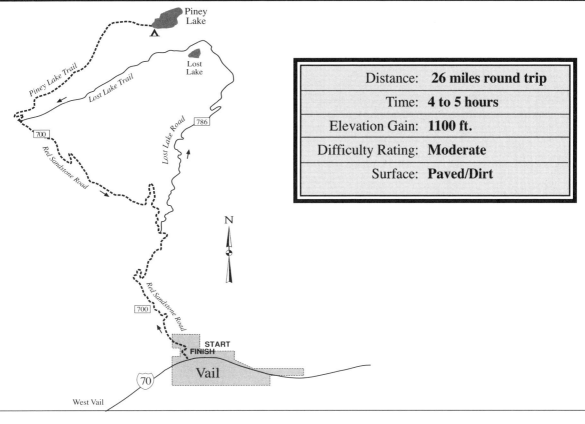

Distance:	**26 miles round trip**
Time:	**4 to 5 hours**
Elevation Gain:	**1100 ft.**
Difficulty Rating:	**Moderate**
Surface:	**Paved/Dirt**

■ Directions: The ride begins at the bikeway in West Vail, at the shopping center on the North Frontage Road.

■ Ride: Ride the bikeway uphill for 1.5 miles until you reach the Red Sandstone Road (FR 700). Turn left here and ride up the paved road and then continue on the dirt road. It is 12 miles to the turn around point at Piney Lake. The ride begins with a steady climb along a high-use, corrugated road. The corrugations decreases as you approach Pinely Lake, but the traffic remains heavy. Since this is such a popular road for motorists, the best times for this ride are weekdays or early mornings.

■ Five miles into the ride, you will pass The Lost Lake 4WD Road. This is another of the popular mountain bike routes in the area. This ride descends for 1.5 miles and then turns upwards again. Take a break at Indian Meadows and enjoy the view of the Gore Range. Continue along the Red Sandstone Road, and you will pass the Red and White Mountain Road, the Lost Lake Trailhead, and the Piney Road. Once past these points the road will begin just past the Piney River bridge switchback down into Piney Valley.

Follow the road to the right, and there are signs marking the way to the Piney Ranch. From where the road forks, it is about two more miles to the lake. Once you get to the lake, take your time to explore the area. The ranch is currently owned by Vail Associates. Respect the rights of others. There is a hiking trail that follows the Piney River Drainage, but it is a Wilderness Area, thus closed to mountain bikers.

Enjoy the peace and beauty here, and rest up for your ride back. It is 13 miles back to West Vail Shopping Center. You will have a few climbs, but it is mostly an easy ride with views of the Vail Mountain Ski Area.

Map: USGS 7.5' Vail West Quad.
Information: White River National Forest, Holy Cross Ranger District, (970) 827-5715.

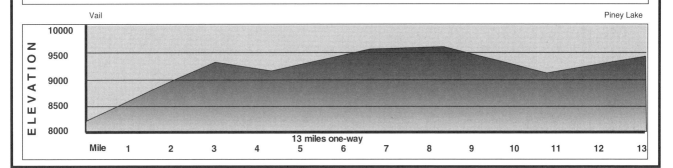

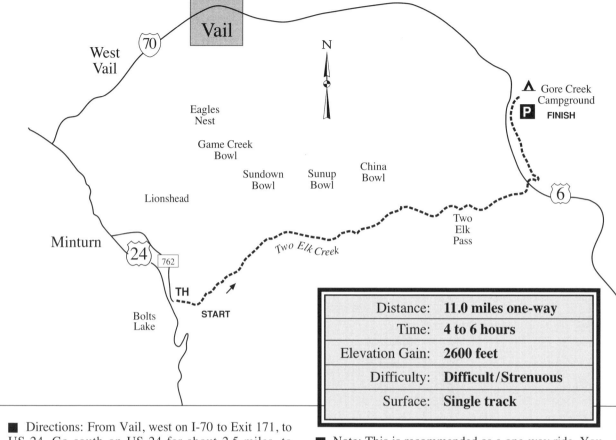

Distance:	**11.0 miles one-way**
Time:	**4 to 6 hours**
Elevation Gain:	**2600 feet**
Difficulty:	**Difficult/Strenuous**
Surface:	**Single track**

■ **Directions:** From Vail, west on I-70 to Exit 171, to US 24. Go south on US 24 for about 2.5 miles, to Cemetery Road. Turn left, crossing the river to FR 762. Turn south and follow the road to where it ends.

■ **Ride:** From the west trailhead, the trail steadily climbs along Two Elk Creek to Two Elk Pass. The trail passes the back bowls of the Vail Ski Area, China Sun-up and Sundown Bowls. From Two Elk Pass it is a challenging descent to US 6. Use the frontage road to return to Gore Creek Campground. The last section is a designated National Scenic Trail that will test your riding skills with rocky sections and many sharp turns.

■ **Note:** This is recommended as a one-way ride. You will need two vehicles for this ride, leave a vehicle at the east trailhead for the return ride to Minturn. The east trailhead is south of I-70 on exit 180, approximately 2 miles south on the frontage road near Gore Creek Campground. Water and restrooms are available at the campground.

Maps: USGS 7.5' Minturn, Red Cliff, Vail East Quads, White River National Forest Map.
Information: White River National Forest, Holy Cross Ranger District, (970) 827-5715.

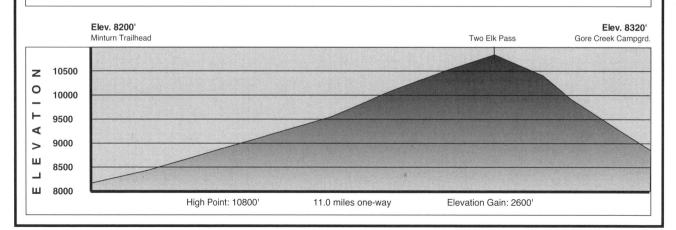

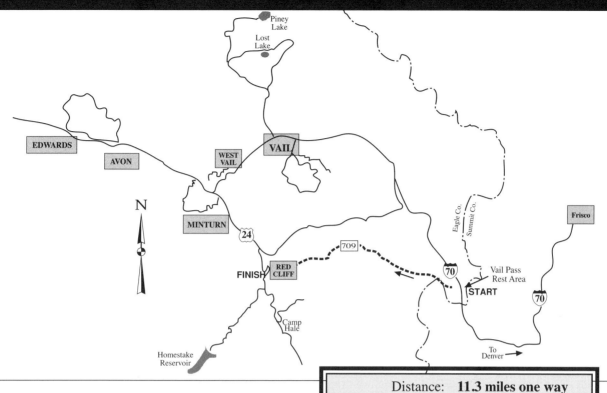

Distance:	**11.3 miles one way**
Time:	**1 to 2 hours**
Elevation Gain/Loss:	**2300 ft.**
Difficulty Rating:	**Moderate/Difficult**
Surface:	**Dirt**

■ Directions: You will need two cars for this ride. Leave one in Red Cliff. For Red Cliff, take 1-70 west to the Minturn-Leadville exit 171. Drive 10.4 miles south on Hwy. 24 to Red Cliff, turnoff before Turkey Creek bridge. Shrine Pass Road (where your ride will end) is the first left, 0.6 mile after turnoff. Do not park on private property in town. Leave the second car at the Vail Pass Rest Area, where the ride begins. To get to the rest area take 1-70 east about 13 miles from the Vail Village Exit.

■ Ride: From the Vail Pass Rest Area, ride up Road #709, the Shrine Pass Road, located at the west side of the rest area. The road pavement ends and the dirt road climbs 2.4 miles up to the summit. There is a road to the left that leads to the Shrine Mountain Inn. To get down to Red Cliff, continue on the Road #709 downhill. It is 9 miles to Red Cliff.

Along the way there is the Mount of the Holy Cross overlook at 3.7 miles. Bear left when you come upon the intersection of Roads #709 and #728, staying on the #709 all the way down. The ride descends through Spruce-Fir forests, and follows Turkey Creek. At mile 7, you will pass an old miner's camp on the left. Finally, you will cross the bridge into Red Cliff at mile 11.3.

Maps: USGS 7.5' Vail Pass and Red Cliff Quads.
Information: White River National Forest, Holy Cross Ranger District, (970) 827-5715.

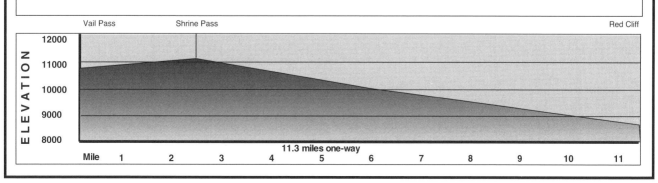

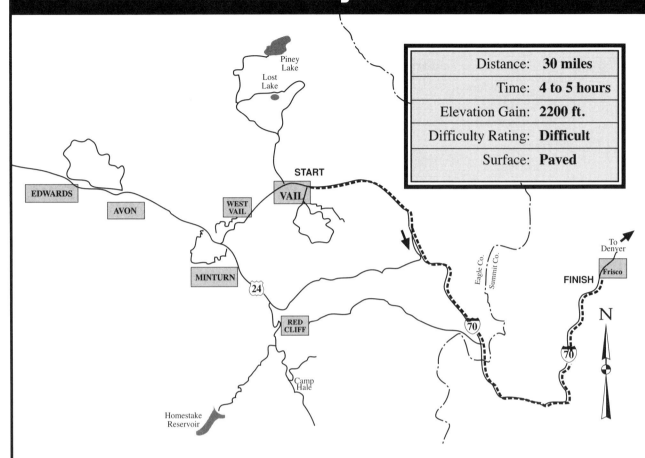

Distance:	**30 miles**
Time:	**4 to 5 hours**
Elevation Gain:	**2200 ft.**
Difficulty Rating:	**Difficult**
Surface:	**Paved**

■ Directions: This 30 mile trail runs from Vail, over Vail Pass, to Frisco. The path ridden in either direction.

■ Ride: The path was dedicated in August of 1980 as a National Recreation Trail. It is paved and approximately seven feet wide. The trail is designed for multipurpose recreation including running and bicycling. It also serves as an access point for fishermen and hunters. In the project's planning stages, cooperative engineering work was done between the U.S. Forest Service and the State Highway Department. The Highway Department now maintains most of the trail.

It should be remembered that the trail is designed for multi-use recreation. We ask that safety be stressed when using the trail. Bicyclists could lose control on the many steep grades and tight corners. The difficulty of the trail is demanding for cyclists in good physical condition.

Maps: USGS 7.5' Red Cliff, Vail Pass and Frisco Quads.
Information: White River National Forest, Holy Cross Ranger District, (970) 827-5715.

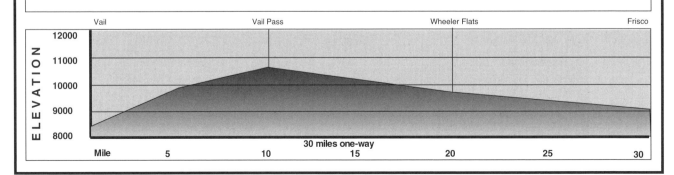

Distance:	**Grand Traverse Trail** **9.0 miles round-trip**
Time:	**1 to 2 hours**
Elevation Gain:	**890 feet**
Difficulty:	**Moderate**
Surface:	**Service road / Single track**

Distance:	**Village Trail** **6.0 miles one-way**
Time:	**1 to 2 hours**
Elevation Loss:	**2150 feet**
Difficulty:	**Easy**
Surface:	**Service road / Single track**

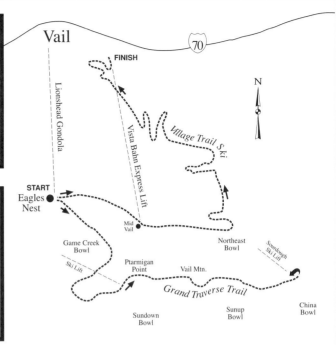

■ Directions: From Vail Village take the Lionshead Gondola to Eagles Nest. Grand Traverse and Village Trails are located on Vail Mountain within the Vail ski boundaries.

■ **Grand Traverse Trail** starts at Eagle's Nest and cuts across the back side of Vail Mountain. It then crosses Game Creek Bowl, and continues on the ridge above the Sundown and Sunup Bowls to the China Bowl. The trail has rolling terrain mixed with ascents and descents of no more than 5% to 7% grades. The landscape varies from meadows to forest.

■ **Village Trail** also starts at Eagle's Nest, as a grad-

ual descent on the service road to Mid-Vail. From Mid-vail join a single track trail, which travels down a fast descent to a service road on a series of switch-backs to Vail Village.

■ Note: There are a number of bike trails on Vail Mountain. The rides range from very difficult to easy. Vail Associates offers mountain bike rentals. Summer operating hours for the lifts are 10:00 am until 4:30 pm.

Maps: Vail and Beaver Creek Resort Mountain Map (Free).
Information: Vail Activities Desk, (970) 476-9090.

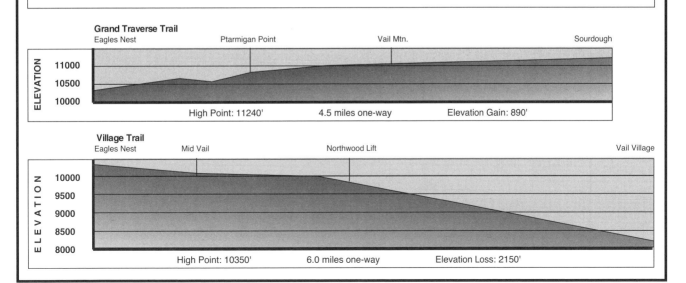

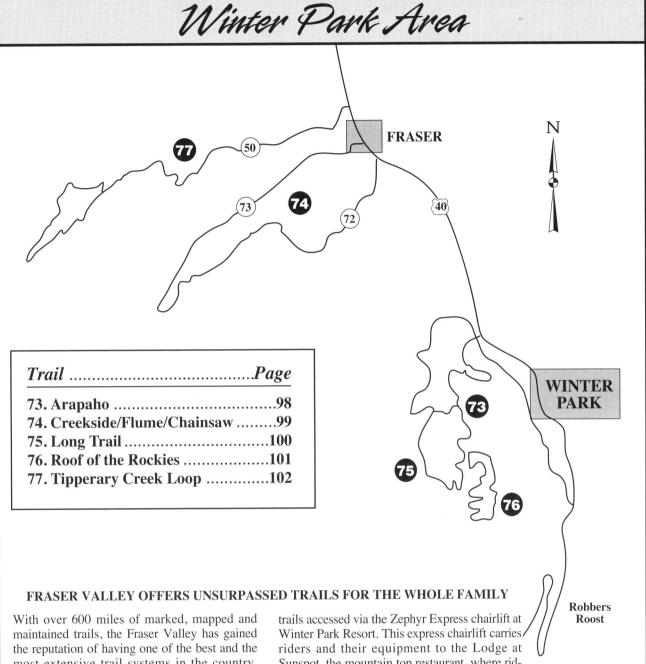

Trail	Page
73. Arapaho	98
74. Creekside/Flume/Chainsaw	99
75. Long Trail	100
76. Roof of the Rockies	101
77. Tipperary Creek Loop	102

FRASER VALLEY OFFERS UNSURPASSED TRAILS FOR THE WHOLE FAMILY

With over 600 miles of marked, mapped and maintained trails, the Fraser Valley has gained the reputation of having one of the best and the most extensive trail systems in the country. Nestled against the Continental Divide, amidst the Arapaho/Roosevelt National Forest, the Fraser Valley offers riders its broad, rolling valley and rugged peaks to explore.

All trails are easily accessible from the heart of Winter Park or Fraser and offer everything from technical single track and old logging roads to challenging ascents and thrilling descents. Trails wind through colorful meadows, aspen glades and lodge pole pine forests as well as allow riders unsurpassed views of the Continental Divide, Indian Peaks Wilderness area and the lush Fraser Valley.

The Fraser Valley trail system is complemented by and connected to the over 44 miles of trails accessed via the Zephyr Express chairlift at Winter Park Resort. This express chairlift carries riders and their equipment to the Lodge at Sunspot, the mountain top restaurant, where riders can access beginner, intermediate or expert trails.

The new Fraser River Trail connects Fraser, Winter Park, and the ski area. Not only does this trail offer an additional and more peaceful way for riders to get from town to town, but it serves as the perfect training ground for true beginners just learning to trust those fat-tire bikes.

Bike rentals are available at the Winter Park Resort base and in town. Guided bike tours leave daily from the center of town and can be tailor-made for any size group or ability level.

■ **Directions:** Arapaho Trail is located within the boundaries of Winter Park Resort ski area.

■ **Ride:** Take the Zephyr Chairlift to Sunspot. Ride the Downhill Trail to the Five Points intersection. At Five Points follow the signs to the start of Arapaho Trail. The trail is a single track with some climbing, difficult switchback turns and rough surfaces. The upper section is rated more difficult and the lower section is rated as most difficult. The dividing line between upper and lower is the crossing of the service road. Lower Arapaho has a section of very difficult switchbacks that will challenge all riders and prepare bicyclists for more difficult rides. The trail ends at the intersection of Upper Cherokee and the Long Trail. Make a right turn here to the Long Trail for the most direct route to the Winter Park base area.

■ **Notes:** Bike rentals are available at Winter Park base. Lift tickets can be purchased in the lower level of the Balcony House. Helmets Required.

Maps: Winter Park/Fraser Valley Mountain Trail Guide (Free).
Information: Winter Park/Fraser Valley Chamber of Commerce, (970) 726-4118.

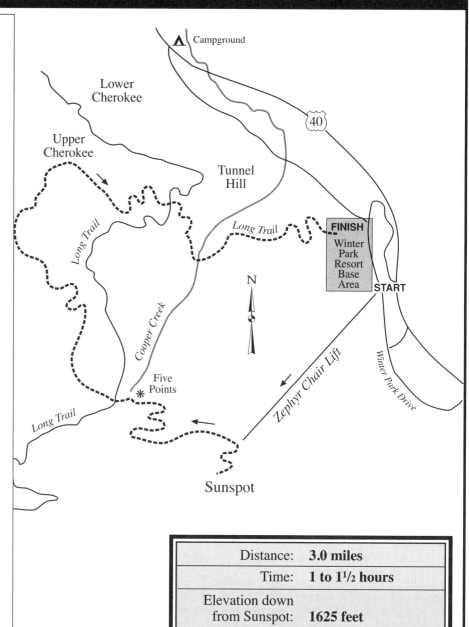

Distance:	**3.0 miles**
Time:	**1 to 1½ hours**
Elevation down from Sunspot:	**1625 feet**
Difficulty:	**More/Most Difficult**
Surface:	**Single track**

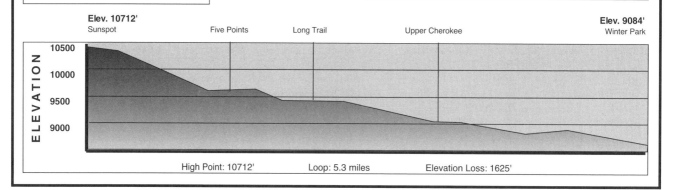

High Point: 10712'   Loop: 5.3 miles   Elevation Loss: 1625'

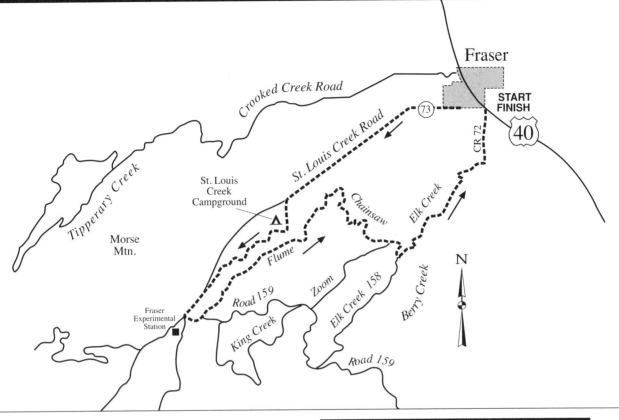

■ **Directions:** Roof of the Rockies is located within Winter Park Resort ski area boundaries.

■ **Ride:** From Fraser, ride west on County Road 73, 2.5 miles to the St. Louis Creek Campground and turn left into the campground. From the campground join the Creekside Trail, a single track trail that follows beside St. Louis Creek. Follow the trail south along the creek, approximately 1.75 miles to FR 159. Turn left, cross the creek, and climb to the Flume trailhead. Two miles north on the Flume Trail you come to a bridge on your left, which crosses the creek to the St. Louis Campground. Past the bridge, the trail becomes the Chainsaw Trail. Continue on this old logging road past Zoom Trail to Elk Creek Road. Turn left on the West Elk Creek Road (CR #72) and return to Fraser. This is a three trail ride with creek crossings, a few steep grades, single track trails and gravel roads.

Distance:	**9.0 mile loop**
Time:	**2 to 3 hours**
Elevation Gain:	**460 feet**
Difficulty:	**More difficult**
Surface:	**Gravel road/Trail**

■ **Note:** This is a scenic ride that passes through several historical sites. Great wildlife viewing.

Maps: Winter Park/Fraser Valley Mountain Bike Guide (Free).
Information: Winter Park/Fraser Valley Chamber of Commerce, (970) 726-4118.

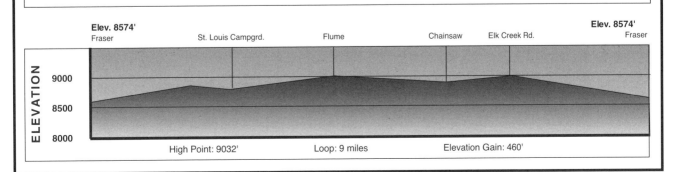

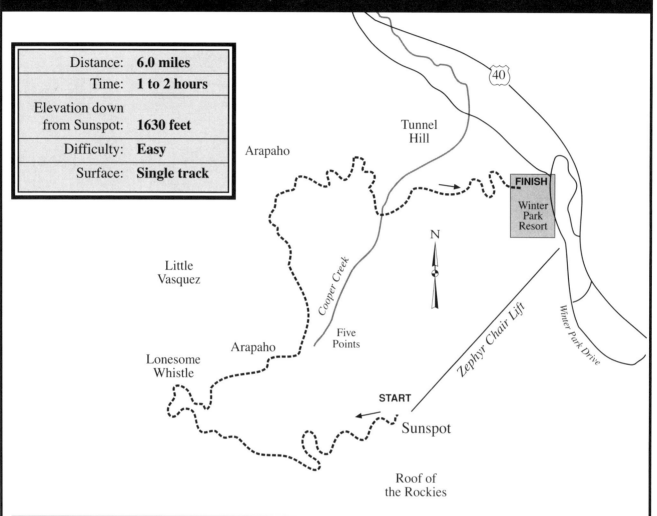

Distance:	**6.0 miles**
Time:	**1 to 2 hours**
Elevation down from Sunspot:	**1630 feet**
Difficulty:	**Easy**
Surface:	**Single track**

■ **Directions:** Long Trail is located within Winter Park Resort ski area boundaries.

■ **Ride:** Take the Zephyr Chairlift to Sunspot, follow the signs to Long Trail. Long Trail is a well maintained, wide, single track trail, with moderate downhills and very few uphills. Long Trail intersects with many other trails located on the Winter Park mountain. Follow the Long Trail signs at intersections and be aware of other trail users. This is a scenic, easy, downhill ride with an good opportunity to view wildlife. Heavy snow can delay the opening of this trail until mid-summer.

■ **Notes:** Bike rentals are available at Winter Park base. Lift tickets can be purchased in the lower level of the Balcony House. Helmets required within ski area boundaries.

Maps: Winter Park/Fraser Valley Mountain Trail Guide.
Information: Winter Park/Fraser Valley Chamber of Commerce, (970) 726-4118.

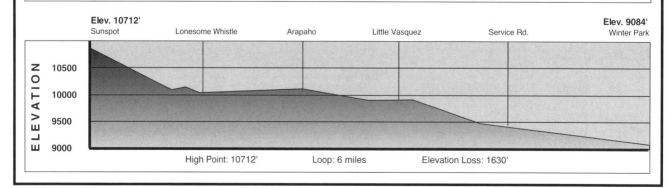

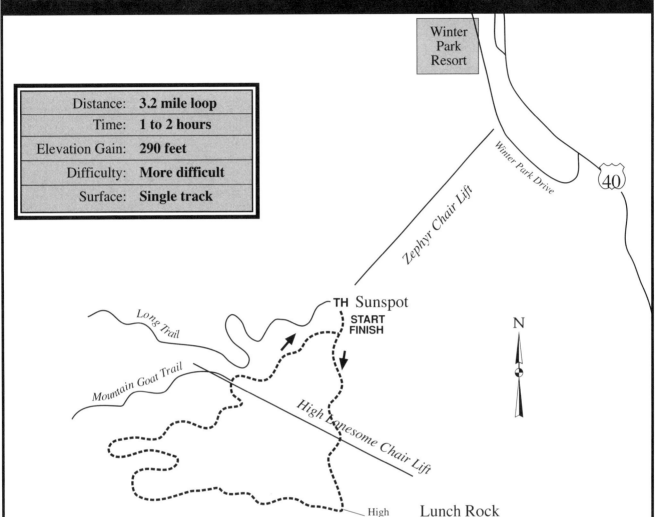

Distance:	**3.2 mile loop**
Time:	**1 to 2 hours**
Elevation Gain:	**290 feet**
Difficulty:	**More difficult**
Surface:	**Single track**

■ Directions: Roof of the Rockies is located within Winter Park Resort ski area boundaries.

■ Ride: Take the Zephyr Chairlift to Sunspot, and follow the signs to the trailhead. This trail is a single track with moderate climbing and rolling downhill sections. The rolling downhill section of Roof of the Rockies winds through high, sub-alpine forest and heavy ground cover. The trail returns to Sunspot on the lower Roof of the Rockies Trail. The high elevation makes the ride more difficult.

■ Notes: Bike rentals are available at Winter Park base. Lift tickets can be purchased in the lower level of the Balcony House. Helmets required within the ski area boundaries. Caution: Be aware of hikers and novice riders on lower Roof of Rockies.

Maps: Winter Park / Fraser Valley Mtn. Trail Guide.
Information: Winter Park/Fraser Valley Chamber of Commerce, (970) 726-4118.

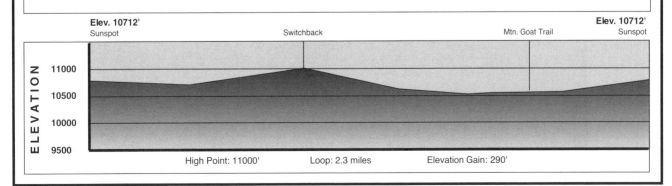

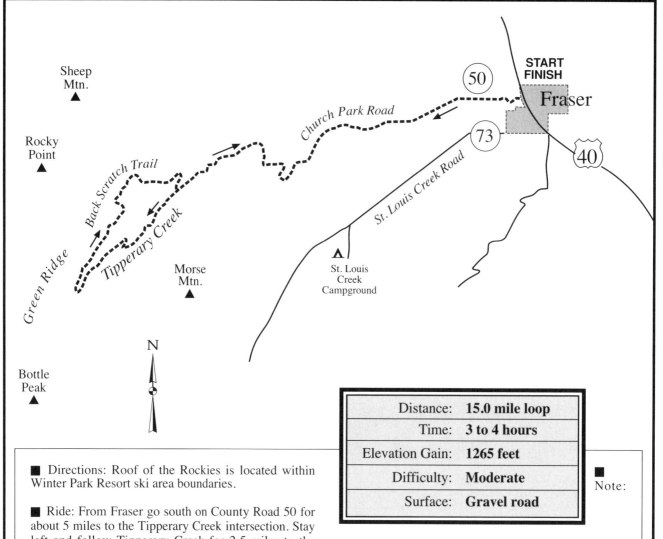

Distance: **15.0 mile loop**

Time: **3 to 4 hours**

Elevation Gain: **1265 feet**

Difficulty: **Moderate**

Surface: **Gravel road**

■ **Directions:** Roof of the Rockies is located within Winter Park Resort ski area boundaries.

■ **Ride:** From Fraser go south on County Road 50 for about 5 miles to the Tipperary Creek intersection. Stay left and follow Tipperary Creek for 2.5 miles to the switchback. This section of the trail is very steep, a 1,000 foot elevation gain in 2.5 miles. At the switchback, make a sharp right turn down a steep grade and ride 1.5 miles to County Road 50. Turn left onto County Road 50 for a 5.5 mile ride back to Fraser. The ride up Tipperary Creek Road will test your stamina.

■ Note:

No drinking water available on the trail.

Maps: Winter Park/ FraserValley Mountain Trail Guide.
Information: Winter Park/Fraser Valley Chamber, (970) 726-4118.

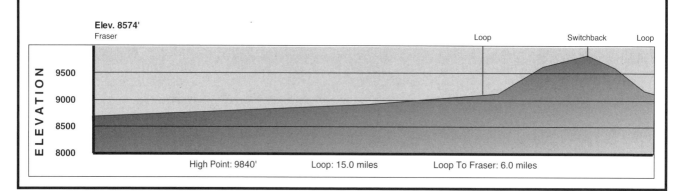

INDEX

Aspen Region Map	7	Lynx Pass	72
Apex Park	36	Matthews/Winter Park	42
Arapaho Trail	98	Meadow Mountain	89
Archuleta Creek	60	Meyers Gulch	19
Berry Creek	84	Mill Creek	90
Bonita Hill	61	Morrison/Tramway Creek Loop	31
Boreas Pass Road	76	Mosquito Lake	65
Boulder Region Map	15	Mount Falcon	43
Buffalo Creek/Colorado Trail	30	Mountain Lion Creek	66
Buffalo Park Road	70	Mountain Lion/Golden Gate State Park	44
Burro Trail/Mayflower Lake	77	New Santa Fe Trail	26
California Gulch	62	Owl Creek Road	11
Camp Hale to Ptarmigan Pass	85	Palmer/Redrock Loop	27
Chatfield Reservoir Loop	37	Peaks Trail	80
Cherry Creek Bike Path	38	Pierson Park	50
Colorado Springs Region Map	25	Piney Lake	91
Colorado Springs/Denver Region Map	29	Pole Hill	51
Creekside/Flume/Chainsaw	99	Rabbit Ears Peak	73
Crosier Mountain	48	Rampart Reservoir	28
Dakota Ridge Trail	39	Red Feather Lakes Loop	57
Davos Trail	86	Red Rocks Trail	45
Denver Region Map	35	Rio Grande Trail	12
Dillon-Keystone Trail	78	Roof of the Rockies	101
Elk Meadow Park	40	Round Mountain	67
Estes Park Region Map	47	Saguache Region Map	59
Fish Creek Falls	71	Sally Barber Mine	81
Foothills Trail	54	Smuggler Mountain Road	13
Fort Collins Region Map	53	Sourdough Trail	20
Fourth of July	16	St. Vrain Mountain Trail	22
Gold Run Gulch	79	Steamboat Springs Region Map	69
Golden Gate Canyon	41	Steamboat to Steamboat Lake State Park	74
Government Trail	8	Stoney Pass	32
Hewlett Gulch	55	Summit County Region Map	75
Homestake Reservoir	87	Switzerland Trail	21
Horsetooth Rock	56	Tipperary Creek Loop	102
House Rock	49	Two Elk	92
Hunter Creek Loop	13	Ute Pass	68
Jamestown	17	Vail Pass Ten Mile Canyon Nat. Rec. Trail	94
Kerber Creek	63	Vail Pass to Red Cliff	93
Lefthand Canyon	17	Vail Region Map	83
Lincoln Creek Road	9	Village Trail and Grand Traverse	95
Little Annie Road Loop	10	Walker Ranch	23
Long Trail	100	Waterton Canyon	33
Lost Lake	88	White Ranch	24
Luder's Creek	64	Winter Park Region Map	97